Travel Guide

INDONESIA

D1252995

JANET COCHRANE
DEBBIE MARTYR

NEW
HOLLAND

NEW
HOLLAND

★★★ Highly recommended
★★ Recommended
★ See if you can

Fifth edition published in 2008
by New Holland Publishers (UK) Ltd
London • Cape Town • Sydney • Auckland
10 9 8 7 6 5 4 3 2

website: www.newhollandpublishers.com

Garfield House, 86 Edgware Road
London W2 2EA, United Kingdom

80 McKenzie Street, Cape Town 8001
South Africa

Unit 1, 66 Gibbes Street, Chatswood
NSW 2067, Australia

218 Lake Road, Northcote
Auckland, New Zealand

Distributed in the USA by
The Globe Pequot Press, Connecticut

ISBN 978 1 84773 102 9

Publishing Manager: Thea Grobbelaar
DTP Cartographic Manager: Genené Hart
Editors: Carla Zietsman, Thea Grobbelaar,
Tarryn Berry, Paul Barnett
Consultant: Janet Cochrane
Design and DTP: Nicole Bannister
Cartographers: Carryck Wise, Nicole Bannister
Picture Researchers: Zainoenisa Manuel,
Shavonne Govender

Reproduction by Hirt & Carter (Pty) Ltd, Cape Town
Printed and bound by Times Offset (M) Sdn. Bhd.,
Malaysia.

All photographs by **Gerald Cubitt** with the
exception of the following:
Philip Game: pages 16, 55;
Jill Gocher: pages 4, 11, 13, 16, 17, 18, 20 (above),
26, 29, 58, 60, 62, 63, 65, 66, 72, 75, 77, 78, 79, 81.
Pictures Colour Library: cover

The publishers, author and photographer
gratefully acknowledge the generous assistance
during the compilation of this book of:
The Directorate General of Tourism, Indonesia
(London and Jakarta). Additional research by
Kelvin Shewry and Andrew Kirkman

Keep us Current
Information in travel guides is apt to change, which
is why we regularly update our guides. We'd be
grateful to receive feedback if you've noted something we should include in our updates. If you have
new information, please share it with us by writing to
the Publishing Manager, Globetrotter, at the office
nearest to you (addresses on this page). The most
significant contribution to each new edition will
receive a free copy of the updated guide.

This guidebook has been written by independent
authors and updaters. The information therein repre-
sents their impartial opinion, and neither they nor the
publishers accept payment in return for including in
the book or writing more favourable reviews of any
of the establishments. Whilst every effort has been
made to ensure that this guidebook is as accurate
and up to date as possible, please be aware that the
facts quoted are subject to change, particularly the
price of food, transport and accommodation. The
Publisher accepts no responsibility or liability for any
loss, injury or inconvenience incurred by readers or
travellers using this guide.

Cover: *Prambanan, Yogyakarta.*
Title Page: *Fishing boat off Cabuhan, West Java.*

CONTENTS

1
Introducing
Indonesia

Most countries offer the foreign visitor an insight into a different culture, but Indonesia, with its dozens of historical influences, offers something dramatically more. The strands of varied customs, religions, legends and modernity are woven into complex patterns that reveal themselves in layers. Visitors with only a few days to spare will find much of colour and vitality to attract them, while those with more time will discover something deeper about the country's subtlety and diversity.

During the 1980s and 90s Indonesia began to attract tourists in large numbers because the government was keen to tap into this useful source of income and did much to reduce some of the factors that deterred tourists in the past. Travel to and around the more remote regions of Papua and Kalimantan may still not be as easy as getting from town to town at home, but it is – generally – no longer something that requires the courage and intrepidity of a wilderness explorer! There has been a vast expansion of flight networks, internet communications have made a huge difference to finding out about destinations and booking accommodation, and the comprehensive network of buses and boats help visitors reach the most distant islands and villages.

Sometimes, when a country is transformed in this way, it pays a heavy price in terms of cultural losses. Not so in Indonesia. For every stretch of silver beach filled with sunbathers from nearby luxury hotels there are plenty of villages rich in traditions that date back not just for centuries but for millennia.

TOP ATTRACTIONS

*** Komodo Island: home of the huge Komodo dragons.
*** Borobudur: the world's largest Buddhist temple; the greatest ancient monument in the southern hemisphere.
*** Mt Bromo: live volcanic crater set amidst a dramatic landscape of lava flows and steep mountain walls.
*** Bali: wonderful for a holiday, combining sunshine, beaches, fantastic hotels and world-class spas with colourful culture.
*** Krakatau Island: the world's most famous volcano, slowly rebuilding itself after the eruption of 1883.

Opposite: *As sun sets, a West Javanese fisherman wades to the shore.*

LAND CONNECTIONS

Some parts of Indonesia have been connected in the past with continental landmasses. Papua was at one stage linked with Australia, while Sumatra, Kalimantan, Java and Bali were connected to the Southeast Asian mainland in the Ice Ages when sea levels were lower. The ancestors of the Australian Aborigines and the Tasmanians almost certainly reached their territories via these land-bridges. Maluku, Nusa Tenggara and Sulawesi have never been connected to a major landmass.

Below: *Indonesia's land-scape has been sculpted by volcanism. This view is across the Sand Sea at Mount Bromo, with Mount Semeru in the distance.*

THE LAND

With an area of about 1,950,000km² (just over 750,000 sq miles), the Republic of Indonesia is the largest country in Southeast Asia and the world's largest archipelago. It stretches some 5150km (3200 miles) and includes over 17,500 islands: about 6000 are inhabited. Roughly 70% of the population lives on **Java (Jawa)**, although with an area of 132,187km² (51,123 sq miles) (approximately the size of England and Wales) this is far from the largest island; the other major islands are **Sumatra** (473,606km²; 183,166 sq miles) and **Sulawesi** (189,216km²; 73,179 sq miles), to which must be added **Kalimantan** (539,460km²; 208,635 sq miles), which is the Indonesian part (about 70%) of the island of Borneo, and **Papua** (421,981km²; 163,200 sq miles), the Indonesian part (about 50%) of New Guinea, known until 2002 as Irian Jaya.

Indonesian landscapes are often rugged. Shallow seas patterned with coral reefs surround shores of mangrove swamps and coastal plains reaching back to dense rainforest. The mountains and geological structures are mainly volcanic, with many of the volcanoes still active, for this is a region of geological turmoil. Indonesia straddles not two but three of the tectonic plates of

the earth's crust, at whose margins there is ceaseless volcanic and earthquake activity: this was dramatically and tragically illustrated by the Asian tsunami in December 2004. New Guinea and the islands around it are on the **Sahul Shelf**, which is properly part of the Australasian plate. Borneo, Java, Bali, **Sumatra**, Lombok and Nusa Tenggara are on the **Sunda Shelf**, which is part of the Asian continental plate; until the Java Sea formed not much over 10,000 years ago there were land connections between the western islands and the

Asian continental landmass. Sulawesi and Maluku belong to the same geological unit as Japan and the Philippines. The junctions between these plates are marked by deep-sea trenches including the famous **Java Trench**, 7450m (24,440ft) deep.

Volcanic Lands

Indonesia is estimated to have 128 active volcanoes. Of these the best known is **Krakatau (Krakatoa)**, an island between Java and Sumatra whose eruption in 1883 coloured skies world-wide for more than a year and sent tsunamis to ravage neighbouring coastlines. The sound of the explosion was heard nearly 5000km (3000 miles) away. The island was literally blown to bits, but is being slowly rebuilt by continuing volcanism.

Other volcanoes of note include **Agung** (in Bali), dormant for nearly a century and a half before its violent eruption in 1963; **Merapi** (near Yogyakarta in Java), whose frequent eruptions are tolerated by local inhabitants because, despite the destruction, they add considerably to the agricultural fertility of the soil; **Bromo** (East Java), with its dramatic scenery and fascinating myths; **Galunggung** (in western Java), whose eruption in 1982 sent a mass of ash into the upper atmosphere and nearly swatted a British Airways passenger plane from the sky; and **Kelud** (near Kediri, also in Java), whose ash-flows can mix with the waters of its crater lake mix to form swiftly moving lahars (mudflows).

Despite occasional eruptions, many of the volcanoes are popular with climbers, including **Merapi**, **Semeru** (the highest mountain in Java), **Rinjani** (in Lombok), Leuser (in Sumatra) and the twin volcanoes of **Pangrango** and **Gede** (in Java). Most cities and universities have active mountaineering clubs, and in Jakarta there is a mountain-climbing group of expatriates and Indonesians called the Java Lava Club.

Above: *Looking across the Sunda Straits at sunset. In any discussion of Indonesia's geography it is important to remember the pervasive influence of the sea.*

THE RING OF FIRE

Indonesia lies in one of the world's most volcanically active areas, at the juncture of several tectonic plates, which gives rise to a pattern of volcanic and earthquake activity around the Pacific Ocean and including Japan, New Zealand and the western coast of the Americas.

Above: *A feral buffalo in East Java's Baluran National Park.*

Rivers and Seas

As an island nation, Indonesia has always been dependent upon the sea for transportation and communication, with rivers also important in the interior of the larger landmasses, notably Kalimantan.

The shallow seas around the archipelago are vital as a source of food, and as a base for the tourist industry. As well as the numerous resorts of Bali, Lombok, Bintan and other areas, there is excellent scuba-diving around North Sulawesi, Southeast Sulawesi, Maluku, Flores, Komodo and Papua – even the heavily used seas around Java and Bali have some good reefs.

Climate

Indonesia's climate is predominantly tropical, the two main influences on it being the archipelago's equatorial position and its situation between the landmasses of Australasia and Asia, which affect the monsoon seasons. Such temperature variations as there are depend more on altitude than on geographical location, with the highest average temperatures (21–33°C; 70–90°F) at sea-level, but much cooler temperatures in the hills and mountains. There is even a glacier in the high mountains of Papua – and, to great excitement, snow was recorded as falling in a village lying at over 2000m (6500ft) in East Java in 1984.

There are two monsoon seasons. The **East Monsoon** (*musim panas* or hot season) lasts from June to September, and is characterized by dry weather and slightly higher temperatures, especially in eastern Java and eastwards through the archipelago. Conversely, the **West Monsoon** (*musim hujan* or rainy season) lasts from December to March and brings heavy rainfall, especially in the western archipelago. Even outside the West Monsoon the **rainfall** is generally high in the western islands – Sumatra and Kalimantan do not really have a dry season at all – and the rain can come with terrific intensity over short periods: daily downpours up to 800mm (31in) have been recorded.

The **humidity** is high, generally 75–100%. Afternoon thunderstorms occur frequently all over Indonesia.

CLIMATE EXTREMES

The wettest area of Indonesia is around Mount Slamet, in Central Java: here the phenomenal average annual rainfall may be more than 7000mm (275in). In the worst recorded storm in Indonesia 800mm (31in) of rain fell in a single day. By contrast, Central Sulawesi's Palu Valley has an average annual rainfall of under 500mm (20in).

However, deforestation in the larger islands has caused a notable shift in climate patterns, with the rainy season starting later than it used to and many areas receiving less rainfall.

Flora and Fauna

The British naturalist Alfred Russel Wallace, who with Charles Darwin realized that the mechanism for evolution was natural selection ('the survival of the fittest'), recognized that there was a difference in the flora and fauna of the islands of the Sunda Shelf to the west, including Sumatra, Java, Borneo and Bali, and the islands to the east, including Sulawesi and Lombok. To the west are Asian mammals such as elephants, monkeys, orangutans, rhinoceroses and tigers, while to the east many of the animals are related to those of Australasia, including marsupials like the kangaroo.

Above: *A green turtle hatchling makes its intrepid way across Sukamade Beach to the sea at Java's Meru Betiri National Park.*

Indonesia has an extremely high level of biodiversity with many species found nowhere else in the world. One of the best known is the **Komodo dragon**, a giant lizard found only on Komodo and Rinca. Other notable species are the **orangutan**, native to Sumatra and Kalimantan, the **Sumatran rhinoceros** and the **Javan rhinoceros**, only 50–60 of which survive. The large **Banteng** ox is also a vulnerable species. Kalimantan has the unique **proboscis monkey**, while Sulawesi has several endemics including the boar-like **babirusa** and the **anoa**, a dwarf buffalo.

Below: *A Javan gibbon in Halimun National Park, West Java.*

With over 1500 species of **bird**, including cockatoos and birds-of-paradise in the east, the country is a mecca for bird-watchers – even though it takes tenacity to visit some of the more interesting bird-watching areas. All visitors are certain to be struck by the variety, ubiquity and size of the **insects** and other invertebrates, many of which are beautiful or extraordinary.

The rainforest has about 40,000 flowering species, from the world's largest flower, *Rafflesia arnoldii*, to tiny orchids. At least 3000 species of tree flourish in the archipelago, many of economic importance, with woods such as teak, ironwood and the pinky-red meranti being valuable commodities. There were estimated to be around 98 million hectares (242 million acres) of forest left in 2002 – but that around 2 million hectares (5 million acres) are disappearing every year.

HISTORY IN BRIEF

The human history of Indonesia can be said to date back at least half a million years, for that is the date ascribed to the hominid fossils found in 1891 by Eugène Dubois on the Solo River in Central Java. Java Man, as the remains were called, was originally allotted by the German zoologist Ernst Haeckel to the genus *Pithecanthropus*, meaning 'ape-man'; once it was established that **Java Man** was part of the ancestral tree of modern human beings, *Homo sapiens*, the fossils were reclassified as belonging to the species *Homo erectus*. In 2004 theories of human evolution were rocked when the remains of 18,000-year-old hominids just a metre high were discovered on Flores: the species has been named *Homo floresiensis*.

Indonesia's history, like everything else about the archipelago, has been profoundly affected by the sea. Waves of human immigration to the islands must have

Below: *Indonesian history seems part of the present. These newly made stone carvings on sale in Bali could have been produced centuries ago.*

occurred from at least 40,000 years ago, since it is thought that humans reached Australia by travelling through the archipelago – although at that time sea levels were lower and there were land-bridges in place of the tricky currents and channels which exist now. From around 3000BC migration increased, with different groups bringing their languages and customs, echoes of some of which still

HISTORICAL CALENDAR

3000BC First waves of immigration by Asian tribes to the archipelago.

AD71 Pliny records Indonesian traders with Africa.

5th cent. Brahman missionaries bring Hinduism to the archipelago.

7th cent. Sriwijaya well established.

8th cent. Sailendra kingdom well established.

c778 onward Borobudur built.

10th cent. Sriwijaya loses trade monopoly with China.

11th cent. Islam arrives in the archipelago.

1268 Kertanagara comes to the throne.

1292 Kertanagara deposed; Marco Polo visits Indonesia.

14th cent. Final extinction of Sriwijayan kingdom.

1602 Dutch East India Company assumes rule of Indonesia.

1799 Dutch East India Company wound up.

1811 British East India Company takes over.

1883 Eruption of Krakatau (Krakatoa).

1891 Discovery of 'Java Man' fossil remains.

1942 Japanese occupation.

1945 Declaration of independence by Sukarno.

1949 Formal transfer of Dutch sovereignty.

1963 Irian Jaya ceded to Indonesia by the Netherlands.

1965–1966 Civil turmoil.

1966 Suharto takes over from Sukarno.

1975 Invasion of East Timor.

Mid-1980s 'Economic liberalization' policies.

1998 Suharto steps down; BJ Habibie becomes president; release of political prisoners; freedom of press.

1999 East Timor regains independence.

1999 President Abdurrachman Wahid elected.

2001 Megawati Sukarnoputri becomes president.

2004 President Susilo Bambang Yudhoyono elected.

survive. For instance, the indigenous tribes of the Mentawaian islands, off the west coast of Sumatra, have cultural similarities with historical groups in Indochina. With different peoples establishing independent settlements all around the coastlines and bringing their own languages, there are now around 580 different languages spoken within Indonesia. (The lingua franca – and official language – is **Bahasa Indonesia**.)

By the second century BC trading links with China were established, and gradually trade with other parts of the world was developed. The first records of this appear to be in the works of Pliny the Elder, whose *Historia Naturalis* (begun after AD71) seems to refer to trade between people from Indonesia and the cultures of eastern Africa. There may have been an Indonesian colony on Madagascar by then, and the Malagasy people of today have physical and linguistic characteristics in common with the Malays of the archipelago. It was about this time that **Hinduism** first came to Indonesia, with the arrival of Indian traders. However, the real impact of

Below: *The monkey god, Hanuman, in a Balinese performance of the Ramayana.*

WORDS THAT REVEAL

There are still living linguistic reminders of the various influences on Indonesia in the form of Indonesian words derived from Sanskrit, Arabic, Portuguese, Dutch and English.

Hinduism was to arrive much later, as a deliberate missionary act by Brahmans, probably in the 5th century AD; by a lucky coincidence, some of the basic ideas of Hinduism accorded with existing Indonesian mountain-worship, and a hybrid of the two religions emerged. As Indonesia's major trading partner at that time was southern China, **Buddhist** influences also began to play a part.

Sriwijaya

Until perhaps the 7th century the peoples of the Indonesian islands retained their multiplicity of comparatively small communities, trading and sometimes fighting with each other. Then, a major Buddhist kingdom, Sriwijaya, established itself with its centre probably just to the west of modern **Palembang**, in Sumatra. The rulers of Sriwijaya amassed considerable wealth as a result of an extensive trade network and use of the region's natural resources. Although the primary religion was Buddhism – largely, it seems, a corrupted form of Tantric Buddhism, using magic for selfish ends – Hindu relics, too, have been excavated from the area, and there is evidence that traditional Malay magical beliefs were also practised.

At the end of the 7th century Sriwijaya moved to conquer the smaller communities along the northeastern coast of Sumatra and thereby monopolize the lucrative trade with China. The maharajahs made various treaties with the natives of smaller islands so that merchant ships could pass unmolested. In this way the kingdom survived until the 10th century, it being convenient for the Chinese to deal with only one centre. However, the Chinese then began trading with local production centres elsewhere in the region, and there was little

Below: *Borobudur, built during the late 8th and early 9th centuries, is the world's largest Buddhist monument.*

Sriwijaya could do to stop them. The kingdom may have dragged on until sometime in the 14th century, but by then its power was a mere husk.

The Sailendra Princes and the Majapahit Empire

Meanwhile, from about the 8th century, central Java had been ruled by the Sailendra princes. The wealth of their small kingdom

was based on agriculture, and they were able to spend lavishly on building religious monuments. In particular, the vast sanctuary and burial edifice of **Borobudur** was built over some 50 years from the end of the 8th century onwards, and the **Temple to Siva at Prambanan** began to be constructed at about the time that Borobudur was completed.

However, historical records show that at about the start of the 10th century there was a sudden cessation in the creation of monuments, inscriptions and other artefacts in central Java. In eastern Java a series of petty kingdoms rose, fractured and disappeared, thanks to turbulent rulers – rulers rather than commoners, for the commoners seem to have desired a stable kingdom if only for the sake of peace. Yet, despite all this upheaval, eastern Java was extremely wealthy because of continuing trade with China, and so Java slowly began to assume a dominant position in the archipelago.

In 1268 the Javanese king **Kertanagara** came to the throne, and within a few years had extended his kingdom to include southern Sumatra's ancient kingdom of Malayu. Through overseas contacts he established himself as the pre-eminent ruler in this part of the world. Like local rulers for centuries before him, he assumed the status of divinity, and his cult freely mixed Buddhist and Hindu elements. He was overthrown and killed in 1292 (the year in which **Marco Polo** visited Indonesia), but not before he had – unwisely – sent the envoy of

Above: *The temple of Tanah Lot on Bali was built by Sang Hiyang Nirarta, one of the last Javanese missionaries to come to Bali.*

AN INDUSTRIOUS PRIME MINISTER

The Majapahit Empire reached its peak during the reign of King Hayam Wuruk as a result of the endeavours of his prime minister, Gajah Mada, who dedicated so much energy to uniting the islands of the region that when he died, four men had to take over his functions. Modern historians believe that the empire's boundaries may have been much more circumscribed than was once thought, with outlying territories linked to Majapahit by trade rather than by sovereignty.

MYSTICAL ISLAM

Just as the Indonesians had earlier adapted Buddhism to their own needs and beliefs, so they accepted Islam very much on their own terms. The form of Islam that came to the islands had anyway been much changed from that in the religion's cradle in Arabia: it had passed through India and taken on mystical aspects there.

Kublai Khan home with his nose cut off and 'No' tattooed on his forehead. By the time a punitive Mongol expedition arrived in Java the usurper himself had been despatched by Kertanagara's son-in-law **Kertarajasa**, who used guile to repel the threat from overseas, then set up his new capital at **Trowulan**, in eastern Java south of present-day Surabaya. Kertarajasa and his successors gradually established dominance over most of present-day Indonesia as well as parts of Malaysia.

The Growth of Islam

The first Arab traders probably arrived in northern Sumatra around the time of the first millennium, bringing Islam with them. It was a mystical strand of Islam known as Sufism, which accorded well with the existing blend of Hinduism, Buddhism and animism to form a peculiarly idiosyncratic type of Islam. By the end of the 13th century there were two small Islamic kingdoms in northern Sumatra. Over the succeeding two centuries, again because of traders, small Islamic kingdoms spread along the northern shore of Java and around Maluku. The impetus seems to have been entirely commercial: local rulers and their subjects initially converted to the new religion in order to enhance trade with the many Muslim cultures in Asia.

There was no centre of Indonesian Islamic culture from which all else spread; rather there were spontaneous growths of the community here, there and everywhere. The scattered nature of the resulting centres of power and influence was to prove a major weakness when the Dutch and other Europeans arrived.

Below: *Near Banten in West Java, a fortress built by 17th-century sultan and national hero Hasanuddin, who waged a long war against the Dutch.*

European Rule

Seeking the source of valuable spices, traders from Europe and the Middle East came to Indonesia once ship-building technology allowed them to travel further afield. The Portuguese established a presence on the Malay Peninsula early

in the 16th century and arrived in Maluku in 1512. They were followed by the British and then the Dutch, who established the **Dutch East India Company** (VOC) in 1602 and effectively governed most of the country until the end of the 18th century through trade and alliances with different rulers. In 1799 the ailing company was wound up by the Dutch Government, its finances deteriorating because of poor management and competing trading links. Control of the country passed to the Dutch government, who held it until independence except for a five-year period (1811–16) when, as a result of European negotiations during the Napoleonic wars, the **British** held the country. **Thomas Stamford Raffles** was appointed Lieutenant Governor and tried to instigate administrative reforms. His system was never put into effect, and the islands reverted to the Dutch after Napoleon's defeat.

Above: Bugis pinisi *boats, as used by the first Islamic traders to come to Indonesia, have hardly changed over the centuries … except that they now have engines.*

The principal interests of the Dutch were still trade-related and despite various rebellions and an increasingly organized local population – especially in Java – they found various means of levying taxes and exploiting their colony's vast natural resources.

Independence

The country remained in control of the Dutch until 1942, when the Japanese occupied the islands. They proved harsh, exploitative rulers who left a lasting memory of dislike. **Sukarno**, jailed by the Dutch for his nationalist activities, had been freed by the Japanese and made a puppet national leader. On 17 August 1945, just before the Japanese surrendered to the Allies, he and a group of fellow-revolutionaries declared Indonesia independent. The Dutch, however, returned to reclaim their colony. Fierce resistance ensued, until at the end of 1949 the Dutch conceded sovereignty over all of Indonesia except Papua, which was only transferred to Indonesia in 1963.

Sukarno had abundant demagogic skills but lacked political and economic shrewdness. His emphasis on ideology and rejection of ties with the West resulted in economic chaos, and by 1965 inflation was running at

FRIENDS ABROAD

Although the expulsion of the Dutch was a triumph for Indonesia's freedom fighters, their brave efforts were assisted by the pressure other countries brought to bear – particularly the USA, which threatened economic sanctions against the Netherlands. Even so, the struggle for Indonesia's freedom, coming so soon after World War II, was, internationally, very much a forgotten war.

THE FIVE PRINCIPLES

The government of Indonesia has promoted a state ideology called the Pancasila or five principles:

• faith in a supreme god
• faith in a just and civilized humankind
• national pride in the unity of Indonesia
• democracy (not the parliamentary form of democracy used by most Western nations but a system based on discussion, persuasion and consensus)
• social justice, whereby all citizens have political, cultural and social equality.

over 500% per annum. After what may have been an attempted Communist coup, up to half a million people were killed in violent civil strife during 1965–66. From the chaos emerged a new leader, **General Suharto**, who remained head of the government until 1998. Sukarno was kept under house arrest until his death in 1970. Suharto ended the confrontation with Malaysia that had persisted through the later Sukarno years, took Indonesia back into the United Nations and came to an accommodation with Papua New Guinea, but in 1975 invaded **East Timor**. After considerable loss of life, the territory only regained independence in 1999 after the end of the Suharto regime.

GOVERNMENT AND ECONOMY

During the 1970s and early 80s Indonesia experienced a period of strong economic growth based on its oil and gas reserves and, to a lesser extent, on exploitation of the forests. The country's Western-trained technocrats implemented a centralized planning system which benefited most sectors of the population in terms of better health and education and higher incomes. After oil prices fell in the mid-1980s the country was forced to diversify its economy – hence the emphasis on tourism.

Below: *Jakarta is where the reins of the nation's government and economy are held.*

But after increasing levels of nepotism and economic shocks, Suharto was forced to resign in 1998. Indonesia now describes itself as the third largest democracy in the world, after elections in 1999 which were, for the first time in over three decades, carried out in an atmosphere of free speech and choice. There have been several general elections since then. The latest was in 2004 when President Susilo Bambang Yudhoyono was elected.

Although economic and social development has been enormous, many peripheral areas have felt excluded, which is one reason for sporadic inter-communal and anti-government violence. An important component of Indonesia's economic growth is the Chinese community, and as a result of their riches they have often been the target of mob violence at times of unrest. A significant source of discontent is now found amongst Islamic groups influenced by a stricter form of Islam emanating from the Middle East. These express their disapproval of the West and un-Islamic behaviour through attacks on tourist facilities and Christian villages.

Above: *Rice terraces in Bali. Agriculture is vital to the domestic economy.*

There are two legislative houses. The 550 members of the **House of Representatives** are also members of the **People's Consultative Assembly**, which is augmented by regional representatives. Elections to the House of Representatives are held every five years, as are presidential elections.

Social Welfare

Community health centres have been set up all over the country, though many people still rely on traditional therapies such as herbal medicine (very popular) and shamanistic medicine. **Housing** has been a priority, with the improvement of slum areas and the erection of cheap accommodation for the poor. Private charitable organizations play their part in running **orphanages, schools for the handicapped** and **old people's homes**.

Economy

Oil and **gas** are responsible for about 40% of export revenues, with manufacturing of electrical appliances and clothing also significant. Exploitation of **agricultural** and **forestry** resources such as plywood, rubber and palm oil employ large sectors of the workforce, while other products such as cocoa, coffee, coconuts, spices, tea and tobacco are all grown in huge quantities. **Tourism** is a significant contributor to national revenues, bringing

---

NEWSPAPERS

The English-language daily *The Jakarta Post* is excellent for news around Indonesia and has a section on events in and around Jakarta. Pick up leaflets at the airport or your hotel lobby and look out for *Jakarta Kini* – a monthly events guide.

CRIME

Violent crime against foreigners is exceptionally rare, but sneak-thieves and pickpockets are common, particularly in Jakarta and Surabaya, and Bali too is developing an unfortunate reputation. Be careful in crowds in big cities or on buses, and carry cash and passports in a body belt. Keep to hand only enough cash for immediate needs.

CASUAL ENCOUNTERS

Visitors who venture out of the major tourist areas should expect to be the subject of gentle curiosity. The often-heard *Dari mana?* and *Mau ke mana?* ('Where are you coming from?'/'Where are you going?') are ritual questions, asked of any stranger. The easiest answer to either question is the equally ritual *Jalan-jalan* ('Just strolling around'). You will often be asked *Sudah bisa makan nasi?* ('Can you eat rice?') as many Indonesians have the idea that Westerners live solely on potatoes and bread.

around US$5 billion into the country in 2005. **Fishing** is an important food source. The **mining** of metals is also significant, the chief ones being nickel, aluminium, copper, iron, tin and silver.

Mismanagement of **forests** means timber reserves are being rapidly exhausted. Shortage of legal timber causes illegal logging even in national parks. Increasingly the government is being pressurized to convert logging forests to huge oil palm or pulpwood plantations rather than allow the forest to regenerate naturally, and devolution since 2001 of responsibility for managing natural resources to provincial level has resulted in loss of even the tenuous central control formerly held by the government.

The unit of currency is the **Indonesian rupiah (Rp)**; in 2007 the exchange rate was about Rp13,000 to the Euro, Rp 18.800 to the UK pound.

THE PEOPLE

Indonesia is the world's fourth most populous nation, with over 235 million people. It contains a colourful assortment of cultures, traditions and people, summed up in the country's motto *Bhinneka Tunggal Ika*, meaning 'Unity in Diversity'. There are more than 100 distinct ethnic groups, and in many cases the only obvious similarity between two citizens is an ability to speak Bahasa Indonesia, the national language; indeed, many people in remote areas are still unfamiliar with it.

Opposite: *Workers on a cocoa estate in East Java.*
Below: *Savu horsemen in Timor. The horses are small but surprisingly strong.*

To compare a Christian Batak farmer from **North Sumatra** with an animist Asmat carver from the swamps of **Papua** is like looking for similarities between a Moroccan carpet salesman and a Lapp reindeer herder – and the geographical distance between their home territories is roughly the same.

There are, however, rough guidelines for the visitor. The people of the western islands – Java, Bali, Sumatra, and the coastal areas of Kalimantan and Sulawesi – are, in the main, **Malays**. Slender and small-boned, with straight dark hair, most, with the exception of the Hindu Balinese, are Muslim. Travel east from Lombok or Sulawesi, however, and the influence of Melanesia begins to become evident. By the time the traveller reaches Maluku and Papua, the population is utterly different from that of the western islands, with people who are darker-skinned, taller and more heavily built than the Malays of the west.

As the Victorian explorer and naturalist **Alfred Russel Wallace** noted, the differences between the peoples of Indonesia are not just physical. In his classic book *The Malay Archipelago* (1869) he described a visit to the Kei Islands in what was then the South Moluccas:

> I now had my first view of Papuans in their own country … had I been blind I could have been certain these islanders were not Malays. The loud, rapid, eager tones … the intense vital activity manifested in speech and action are the very antipodes of the quiet, unimpulsive Malay. Schoolboys on an unexpected holiday would give but faint idea of the exuberant enjoyment of these people.

BASIC MANNERS

- Losing your temper is loss of face, especially in Java. Be firm, but don't lose your cool – even with school children wanting to practise their English.
- The left hand is used in ablutions and is thus considered unclean. Never offer your left hand in greeting or when giving money or food – train yourself to pass things with your right hand.
- Most Indonesians do not use knives and forks for eating except in Western restaurants – they use spoons and forks instead. In rural areas people generally eat with the fingers (of the *right* hand!).
- Indonesians appear intensely curious to Westerners. You can expect to be quizzed about how much you earn, whether you are married, how many children you have, even what form of contraceptive you use. Don't be offended: the questions are part of the ritual of socializing.

Key players in the mosaic of Indonesian peoples are the **Chinese**. Immensely successful in business – from small shops to huge trading conglomerates – they can be compared with the Jews of pre-war Central Europe and, like the Jews, have suffered periodic discrimination and violence. Until liberalization of the media after the end of the

Above: *A traditionally dressed warrior on Nias Island looks anything but warlike ... although this could soon change.*

TWO LANGUAGES

Most Indonesians speak their own local language and Bahasa Indonesia. Children may not start learning Indonesian until they go to school, although increasingly people just use this.

Suharto regime, for instance, publications in the Chinese script were banned.

Nowadays the once clear-cut differences between the peoples of the various islands are being eroded as the government works to build a national identity. A standardized education system, television, greater ease of moving around the archipelago, and **migration** (both government-sponsored and spontaneous) between overcrowded Java and Bali to less populated islands have all played their part. Children increasingly learn Indonesian as their first language rather than their regional or tribal tongue, to the extent that scholars worry about the loss even of formerly prominent languages such as Sundanese, the native language of western Java.

Tribal Groups

Primitive aboriginal tribes, the original settlers of the archipelago, survive in remote forested areas. Seminomadic hunter-gatherers, they include the **Kubu** and **Sakhai** of Sumatra and the **Wana** of Central Sulawesi. Most are now threatened with the loss of their hunting grounds through deforestation and transmigration projects.

Proto-Malay settlers came to the archipelago at least 3000 years ago, retreating inland and to the highlands when later waves of Malay settlers arrived. Major proto-Malay tribes include the **Batak** of Lake Toba in North Sumatra, the **Torajans** of South Sulawesi and the **Dayaks** of Kalimantan. The Dayaks are found mainly in the east and centre, some still living deep in the interior in longhouses along major rivers.

Papua is home to scores of distinctive tribal groups. Darker-skinned, more heavily built and generally with tightly curled hair, the Papuans include the **Dani** of the highlands around the

Baliem Valley, who became known to the outside world only in the late 1930s, and the **Asmat**, wood-carvers living in the swampy plains of the southern coast.

Orang Laut, or sea gypsies, are found all over eastern Indonesia, living on boats or in stilted settlements on the seashore. Orang Laut people traditionally did everything at sea in their boats – including giving birth.

Religion

Almost all the great religions are represented among Indonesia's myriad peoples and islands, the nation's diversity extending from this world to the next. With the largest population of **Muslims** of any country, Indonesia is also the most easterly stronghold of **Hinduism** and home to the world's greatest Buddhist monument (Borobudur – *see* page 64) and some of the oldest **Christian** churches in Southeast Asia.

The importance of religion in Indonesia cannot be overestimated. Belief in one supreme God is the first statement of **Pancasila**, the five principles which form the core philosophy of modern government in Indonesia, and is part of the glue that holds together – if loosely – a nation of enormously disparate people. Catholicism, Protestantims, Islam, Hinduism and Buddhism are all recognized equally by the government.

As practised in Indonesia, the religions have their own national flavour. Here, perhaps more than anywhere else in the world, religions born of other nations have been accepted and reconciled with animist beliefs which date back to the earliest days of humankind. In **Java** devout Muslims make offerings to **Nyai Loro Kidul**, Goddess of the Southern Seas, and the stories of the Hindu epic *Ramayana* are as well known as the *suras* (chapters) of the Koran. In **Sulawesi** and **Sumba**, Christian villagers stage lavish feasts and sacrifices to send their dead into the afterworld with appropriate honour. Even the Hindus of **Bali** have adapted their religion to encompass more ancient beliefs.

THE MUEZZIN'S CALL

In Indonesia, as in any Muslim nation, believers are expected to pray five times daily. Not all do, of course, but this does not prevent the Imam from calling the faithful to prayer in the early hours of the morning. When you book into a guesthouse, first check the location of the nearest mosque – or you risk an early-morning alarm call.

Opposite bottom: *Workers in one of the rice paddies of West Java carry out their labours just as countless generations have done before them.* **Below:** *The 16th-century Masjid Agung Mosque at Banten. The architecture shows both Islamic and Hindu influences.*

MISSIONARIES

Christian missionaries continue to be active in remote areas, notably in Central Sulawesi, Kalimantan and Papua. The flights operated by the Missionary Aviation Fellowship (MAF) are often the only way to reach truly remote settlements. Many of the missionaries are Americans, Europeans or Australians, although growing numbers are Indonesians.

YOUR RELIGIOUS VIEWS

If you fall into conversation with local people you're likely to be asked your religion. Don't mutter about agnosticism or atheism: such viewpoints are incomprehensible in a nation where identity cards carry the bearer's religion. If you are not a member of any of the major religions, it is best to pretend that you are.

Below: *A Roman Catholic shrine on Kei Kecil.*

The dominant religion in Indonesia is **Islam**, which is becoming closer to the puritanical model of the Middle East, with orthodox Islam prevailing in Sumatra's Aceh province and in Buginese areas and, increasingly, in Java. On a day-to-day level, female clothing is now far more conservative than it was a decade ago, with the majority of women now covering their hair in public.

Another major Indonesian religion is **Balinese Hinduism**, aspects of which might not be recognized by the more orthodox Hindus of India. It was to Bali that the priests and nobles of Java's Hindu empires fled in the 16th and 17th centuries from an ascendant Islamic state; meanwhile groups of the peasantry retreated to the mountains of eastern Java, where an archaic form of Hinduism still survives in villages of the Tengger region around Mount Bromo.

Christianity is mainly concentrated in the more remote corners of the archipelago, although there is also a significant Christian presence in Java. Some strong Christian areas – the Batak area of north Sumatra, Ambon, Flores and the Minahasa region of North Sulawesi – were converted by early colonial venturers. Other Christian areas – the interior of Kalimantan and Papua, the mountains of Tanah Toraja – were either too inaccessible or too dangerous to penetrate until the last few decades, but from the 1930s onwards missionaries have been active there.

Religion by Regions

Sumatra is almost 100% Muslim, with Aceh the most strongly Islamic province. Most of the Batak people of the Lake Toba region are Christian. The Dayak tribes of northern and eastern **Kalimantan** are generally Christian, while coastal dwellers in this province are mainly Muslim.

Java is almost entirely Muslim, at least nominally: many Javanese have strong beliefs in spirits and practise a form of meditative spiritualism; they are particularly influenced by pre-Islamic beliefs in the centre and east of the island. Influential Javanese are trying to foster traditional Javanese beliefs as a way of countering the influence of strict Islamic preacers. The reticent Badui of West Java practise an ancient form of Buddhism, while the Tenggerese of Mt Bromo are Hindus, the last practitioners of a religion which once dominated the island.

Bali is Hindu, although with pockets of Islam in coastal villages. **Lombok** is mainly Muslim, with a small population of Hindus of Balinese descent. The southern part of **Sulawesi** is a stronghold of Islam, while the Torajan highlanders of the centre are Christians. The Minahasa of North Sulawesi are generally Christian.

Above: *Balinese women and children taking votive offerings to their temple.*

Northern **Maluku**, notably Ternate and Tidore, are Muslim; the southern islands are Christian and Muslim. The Lesser Sundas (Nusatenggaara) have strongholds of both Islam (Sumbawa) and Christianity (Flores and Sumba). In **Papua** most of the tribes of the interior are now nominally Christian after years of proselytizing by missionaries, although long-established coastal towns are mainly Muslim due to trading influences.

Ramadan

Ramadan, the fasting month, is integral to Islam in Indonesia as elsewhere in the Muslim world. From dawn to dusk, Muslims may not drink, eat or smoke. During this time, restaurants in rural or orthodox Muslim areas are likely to be closed. Visitors should behave with some sensitivity – eating or smoking in the street, for instance, is not advised. Events such as dance and theatre performances may be cancelled.

Ramadan culminates in the great Idul Fitri or Lebaran celebrations, a time of hospitality and visiting, when it can seem as if every Muslim in Indonesia is on the move. It is best to try and avoid traveling at this time, as all forms of transport are extremely crowded, seats on planes and trains are hard to obtain, and prices are steeper than normal. The Islamic calendar depends on the phases of the moon and Ramadan moves forward by 10–11 days each year: in 2007 the first day of Ramadan fell on 17 September.

AT THE MOSQUE

Visitors are generally welcome in Indonesia's many mosques, or *mesjid*. Dress with respect and cover your head if you are a woman.

WOMEN'S ROLE IN SOCIETY

Women in Indonesia enjoy greater freedom than in almost any other Muslim nation. Even in heavily Islamic areas like Aceh there is no tradition of purdah, although an increasing number of women cover their hair with a scarf and wear long-sleeved clothing. Segregation of the sexes is confined to the mosque, and one of the country's most important national holidays, Kartini Day, honours an early Javanese campaigner for women's rights.

LONGHOUSES

Found throughout Borneo, longhouses were – and are – uniquely suited to the local climate and culture. Raised high off the ground for ventilation and, in the past, for defence, these structures can be well over 100m (110yd) long and home to dozens of families. Within the building each family has its own apartment, with areas for cooking, sleeping and eating. Outside, a long, covered veranda, often beautifully painted and carved, provides a communal area where rice is pounded, children play safely and the elderly sit and watch the world go by, protected from rain and sun. The buildings are often fronted by totem poles, 6m (20ft) or more high and carved with fierce warrior figures designed to scare away evil spirits. Some figures boast massive erect phalluses, as jungle spirits apparently do not like sexual arousal.

Staying in a longhouse is an unforgettable experience, but sleep is hard to come by. Pigs and chickens root around underneath, rice is pounded before daybreak, children shriek and hunting dogs howl. The din is astonishing.

ARTS AND CULTURE

One reason for Indonesia's variety of artforms is the country's position at the crossroads of Asia and Melanesia. From Asia come the traditions of Hinduism and Buddhism with their attendant imagery, often superimposed upon a much older tradition of art and religion springing from animist beliefs. The fierce carvings of the Asmat of Papua and the intricate totems of the Dayak of Kalimantan represent the complicated relationships between spirits and nature, with shapes often heavily stylized into a symbolic form of cloud or tree or god, and representations of the cosmic division into upper world and lower world.

With such great distances between different islands and their peoples, cultural unity could hardly be expected. Indeed, such is the difficult terrain in some parts of Indonesia that fascinating differences occurred between groups living just kilometres apart. Until at least the 1930s, for instance, the peoples of Central Sulawesi made cloth from tree-bark because the mountains and thick forests surrounding them were barriers to trade with neighbouring tribes, and woven textiles were unknown. Even now when television, planes, the internet and other forms of communication have helped unify the country, the different ethnic groups retain and develop their unique traditions and arts, and are encouraged to do so by the government.

Textiles

Few visitors to Indonesia leave without buying a locally made textile, whether clothing, tablecloths, pictures or just a length of material. Central Java is particularly well known for its **batiks**, produced by stamping or drawing patterns in wax on fine cotton and then dyeing the cloth. The Lesser Sundas, particularly Sumba, are where Indonesia's other internationally known textile technique – *ikat* – originates. *Ikat* means 'tie', and the threads are wound onto a frame and tie-dyed before being woven on a backstrap loom. Although the vegetable dyes used in the past for most textiles are now rare, the same earthy colours of dull red, blue and brown are still popular.

Performing Arts

Throughout Indonesia the important life-stages, especially marriage and death, are celebrated in music, song and dance. Most islands of western and central Indonesia have bronze gongs, bamboo flutes and simple stringed instruments. The most sophisticated orchestras are in Java and Bali, where groups of up to 30 players combine the percussive sounds of metallophones, drums and gongs with one or two flutes, stringed instruments and the human voice. The whole melodic ensemble is known as the *gamelan*.

Above: *Traditional Balinese wood carvings on sale in the street.*

The *gamelan* forms the musical backdrop to performances of **dance** or **puppetry**, generally re-enacting the stories of Hindu mythology. The music, dance and drama of Bali are perhaps the most attractive to the casual visitor because of their vitality, glittering colours and dynamic rhythms, while in Central Java the grace of the court dancers and the incredible skill of the master puppeteer manipulating his shadow puppets should not be missed. Indeed, the interest of tourists is helping to maintain these art forms.

Carving and Metalwork

Carving in wood or stone and working metals like bronze, silver and gold are centuries-old crafts known throughout the archipelago. Examples of neolithic stone-working can be seen in the tombs of the Lesser Sundas or the statues of Central Sulawesi, while the fanciful carvings still made for Balinese temples echo the reliefs on the thousand-year-old temples of Java. The techniques of wood carvings stretch from the coastal swamps of Papua to the mountains of Sumatra, where villagers decorate their clan houses with carved and coloured panels.

At celebrations Indonesia's peoples bedeck themselves in particular finery. Examples of the colourful beadwork of Kalimantan can be seen in museums or handicraft shops in Jakarta, and most provincial museums hold fine gold or silver regalia. The silver ornaments of Yogyakarta, still beautifully crafted using

TOURIST PERFORMANCES

Don't miss the skilful performances of dance, music and puppetry put on for tourists. Indonesians are justifiably proud of their culture and mostly present it to a very high standard. The performances are shortened for Western tastes, but are none the worse for this. Not many tourists are prepared to sit through a traditional all-night performance of Javanese shadow-puppetry – and in fact Indonesians themselves are now much less likely to do so, so that moves are afoot to repackage performances for the domestic market too.

'ANTIQUES'

Indonesia's craftsmen and merchants have long realized that overseas visitors will pay top prices for antiques. Entire villages busily turn them out – like Mojokerto in East Java, which produces wonderful replicas of 13th-century Majapahit vases and jugs. Usually this is done simply to cater to market tastes for old-style ornaments rather than to deceive.

Art-lovers seeking to buy genuine Asmat carvings should exercise caution – there are large numbers of fake pieces produced in Java or Bali on the market. In 1993 Asmat carvers tried to take legal action against one Javanese village for breach of copyright!

ancient techniques, make excellent souvenirs – easier to carry home than a full-size bronze gong!

Crafts and Shopping

Indonesia's long history and its range of cultures come to dazzling life in the teeming markets and fascinating craft villages. Many traditional crafts are deeply rooted in the culture of their island of origin. To appreciate them to the full, it is most rewarding to buy from the region where they are produced rather than from a souvenir shop in Java or Bali – although for people without the time to visit remote regions of the country, the government-sponsored handicraft stores have excellent examples from all over the archipelago at reasonable prices. The simplest craft items are found in the markets: a woven basket for winnowing rice, a bamboo flute, a long-handled rice spoon or a plain earthenware bowl.

Bargaining

If a shop has price tags on its goods it's likely to be a *harga pas*, or fixed-price establishment, as with the majority of department stores. If there are no price tags, prepare to bargain – for everything from earrings to a four-poster bed (it's worth trying this even if there is a price-tag). Where possible, try to establish in advance a reasonable price for the item you hope to buy – your hotel may help. Otherwise consult fixed-price establishments or government-run craft centres for a guide price. Bear in mind that hotel shops tend to be very expensive, and if prices are quoted in US dollars they will be higher than the rupiah price.

If interested in an item, casually ask about it. The trader will normally quote a price. Look horrified and reel backwards muttering *Mahal, mahal!* ('Expensive, expensive!'). Come back with an offer perhaps 30% of the trader's price, and then settle down to business. Beware of 'over-bargaining', i.e. driving the price down too far – sometimes, especially towards the end of the day, traders will settle for a low sum just to have enough cash to buy food for their children.

Below: *A Javanese market offers all sorts of exotic delicacies for the jaded palate.*

Where to Buy It

Java

Jakarta is strong on clothes, last-minute presents and antiques – many of which are newly fabricated! In Indonesian, the word *'antik'* simply means that something is made in an old-fashioned style, and there are now extremely few genuine antiques around. **Yogyakarta** has

carvings, silver, leatherwork, batik and *wayang* puppets. **Solo** has puppets, batik, carving and pottery.

Sumatra

Medan has a good range of crafts (lots of Batak items), including some imports from Kalimantan. **Padang** has palm-leaf basketry and weaving. You might find beautiful, simple wooden bowls and dishes from Siberut. **Kota Gedang (Bukittinggi)** has filigree silver.

Kalimantan

Samarinda is good for antique Chinese ceramics, fantastic Dayak carvings and crafts, and beautiful silk sarongs. **Banjarmasin** is best for precious and semi-precious stones, with a great range of stones, from garnets to diamonds.

Bali

One of the craft capitals of Southeast Asia, making silverware, carvings (wood and stone), paintings, masks and more. **Kuta** is Fashion City – arrive in a T-shirt and leave with a complete wardrobe. Many European designers work from Bali and their designs appear in Kuta shops a season before they arrive in the West.

Lombok

Most of the same crafts as Bali, but with the addition of some attractive heavy pottery and wonderful weaving (sensational curtaining and upholstery material).

Sulawesi

Makassar is good for silver and gold filigree jewellery and brightly coloured silks. **Rantepao** stocks bead

Above: *A Balinese handicrafts shop unashamedly aims its wares at tourists.*

CREATIVE BARGAINING

Bargaining can take some time, with each side modifying the price by degrees. Treat it as fun, and hope to conclude a deal at not more than half the first price – experts will go for one-third, but for that you need time on your hands. Be sure you really want the item before you start bargaining – it is bad manners to reach a mutually agreeable price and then not buy. If bargaining gets sticky, try just walking out – if the owner stops you, a deal has been made. But don't lose a lovely piece of jewellery or weaving for the sake of a few rupiah, and don't be unreasonable: the person you're buying from may need that money to feed her children.

HOT DRINKS

Some of the best **coffee** in the highlands of Sumatra and Java, and good **tea** is also produced. Both tea and coffee are drunk without milk and very sweet; if you don't want sugar added to your tea or coffee, tell the waiter you want it served *pahit* (bitter). Outside major hotels don't expect real **milk** if you ask for it with your coffee or tea: it will usually be sweetened condensed milk.

jewellery and wall-hangings, carved wooden panels and ebony-handled knives.

Nusa Tenggara

Most of the Lesser Sundas produce unique woven fabrics.

Food and Drink

Indonesian food, especially in Java and Sumatra, can be rather spicy to unaccustomed Western palates; the hottest of all comes from the **Padang region** of West Sumatra, served in restaurants all over the archipelago. In general, the further east you travel the less spicy the food, but beware of lurking chilli peppers everywhere. If you are caught, don't reach for water: plain boiled rice, a slice of cucumber or a banana is much more effective.

Rice is the essential food throughout most of Indonesia: eaten boiled or fried and in enormous quantities, it takes the place of both bread and potatoes. Moving east into Maluku and Papua, **cassava**, **sweet potatoes** and **sago** take over as staples, although rice is generally still available.

Below: *This village market in Bali could hardly be more traditional.*

For most Indonesians **meat** is rather expensive and is usually eaten only in small quantities. Typically, a meal might consist of two or more vegetables and a fish, meat

or chicken dish, together with a hot chilli sauce (*sambal*) or pickled vegetables. Chicken and goat are common foods all over the archipelago. For obvious reasons, pork is rarely found in Muslim areas except in Chinese restaurants. **Fish**, eaten fresh or dried, is the major source of protein for tens of millions of Indonesians. Many Javanese dishes contain tofu (*tahu*) or *tempeh*, a delicious nutty 'cake' made from soya beans – perfect for vegetarians.

Coconut oil and coconut milk are used in curries and many sauces, along with lemon grass, ginger, cumin, turmeric, coriander and galangal. In Sumatra and Java, especially, tiny dried fish and chilli peppers are pounded into a paste and added to dishes to intensify the flavours.

Although each region has its own specialities, some dishes extend across the archipelago. Fried rice and fried noodles (nasi goreng and mie goreng) are found everywhere. Originally from Java, gado gado – a cooked vegetable salad in a peanut sauce – is also widely available. Chicken or goat satay, barbecued over a charcoal brazier and served with a peanut sauce, can be bought on almost every street corner.

Regional specialities abound – although not all might appeal. A Batak speciality from North Sumatra is the part-digested cud of water-buffalo, while the Minahasa of North Sulawesi enjoy the meat of dog, fruitbat and rat. Throughout Maluku and Papua sago grubs are a prized delicacy, while Balinese children enjoy roasted dragonfly.

Elsewhere the exoticism is more acceptable to Western palates. In Tanah Toraja try buffalo meat baked in bamboo tubes, or roast suckling pig in Bali. In Samarinda, East Kalimantan, ask for the huge prawns. For a real taste of Indonesia, try eating at one of the food stalls (warungs) which spring up at dusk in every town and city – but stick to what is freshly cooked.

If for no other reason, it is worth visiting Indonesia simply to sample the fruit. Bananas come in dozens of varieties, while mango, papaya and pineapple taste quite different when they have ripened naturally. Don't miss the hairy red rambutan, or the mangosteen, with its luscious melting flesh inside a hard burgundy shell. Most infamous is the huge, thorny durian, banned from planes and hotels because it smells like badly blocked drains. But don't be put off. The creamy flesh tastes like a buttery egg custard with hints of a rich Madeira, onions, cream cheese, liver pâté ... and more. Be warned – you risk becoming an addict!

Above: Luscious – and, most important, cooling – fresh fruit on sale in the streets of Jakarta.

COLD DRINKS

Alcohol is widely available in the form of beer – usually served tepid except in the tourist restaurants. In the main cities and tourist centres you will also find spirits, but the Indonesian-made ones are dire. Australian wines are available in Bali and Jakarta (although a moratorium on wine imports in 2007 caused shortages for the tourism industry). Ice is made in government-controlled factories from purified water and rarely causes illness, though most tourists avoid it. Drink only freshly boiled or bottled water – the many brands widely available are all known as Aqua. For a really thirst-quenching drink, try young coconut juice straight from the coconut (jus kelapa muda). Add rum for a tropical cocktail.

2
Sumatra

The fifth-largest island in the world, Sumatra spans more than 1700km (1050 miles) from northwest to southeast, and accounts for a quarter of Indonesia's total landmass. It is an island of immense forests, extensive mangrove swamps and towering volcanoes, of fascinating cultures, wonderful wildlife and cosmopolitan cities.

The most popular destination is the vast **Lake Toba** in North Sumatra, homeland of the Batak people. To the west are the **Nias Islands**, with their astonishing stone mega-liths, sandy beaches and massive longhouses. Further south are the **Minangkabau Highlands**, where the Minang, a matriarchal group who are also devout Muslims, live in some of the loveliest traditional houses in Indonesia.

Sumatra is justly famous, too, for its wildlife, now protected in national parks like **Gunung Leuser, Kerinci Seblat** and **Way Kambas**. Indigenous animals include orangutan, elephant, rhinoceros, tiger and the Sumatran crocodile. In the forests huge trees festooned with vines and epiphytes rise 30m (100ft) or more from the forest floor, and in the mountains behind the west coast it is possible to see the parasitic rafflesia, the largest flower in the world.

Although some of Sumatra's cities are rapidly expanding and industrializing, most of this vast island remains an adventure to visit, with people living tradi-tional lifestyles based on agriculture and even hunter-gathering. Most Sumatrans are Muslims, although the Bataks of Lake Toba and Berastagi and most Nias Islanders are Christians.

CLIMATE

Sumatra straddles the equator, and the monsoon period in the north differs from that in the south. In the north the rainiest time is from Oct until Mar or Apr, and the dry season runs May–Sep. In the south the monsoon period also starts in Oct, but in Dec–Feb the rains are truly torrential. The best time to visit is towards the end of the dry season. In recent years (in the dry season) the skies have been clogged with haze generated by illegal fires used to clear the forest.

Opposite: *A fisherman's seasonal dwelling.*

Sumatra

DON'T MISS

*** Samosir Island: the Toba Batak here have traditional villages with splendid tombs and megaliths.

** Leuser Ecosystem: over 100 mammal species and 300 bird species are protected here.

** Kerinci Seblat National Park: dominated by an active volcano and has the beautiful Lake Kerinci.

* Bohorok Orangutan Centre: see the great apes at close quarters.

NORTH SUMATRA
Medan

First-time visitors to Indonesia who arrive in Medan should prepare themselves for the fourth largest city in Indonesia, a noisy industrial giant with few obvious charms. It has become particularly frenetic since accommodating the flow of aid money and workers generated by the 2004 tsunami which devastated the northwest coast of Sumatra. As an important regional hub for trade throughout Sumatra and Malay peninsula, it has several buildings reflecting the wealth of both colonial and post-independence times. The Maimoon Palace, built in 1886, was the former home of the Sultanate of Deli, and the nearby Grand Mosque (1906) is attractive and can be visited. The Central Post Office and the Harrison & Crosfield building are both fine examples of Dutch architecture.

Medan has the largest Indian quarter of any Indonesian city (Kampung Keling), with a Hindu temple ornamented in riotous colour, built in 1884. It also has a large Chinese population, and the Taoist temple, also intricately decorated, is the largest in Sumatra. The North Sumatra Museum has replicas of traditional Batak houses and a good display of tribal artefacts. The Zoo, which opened on a new and larger site in 2005, is worth a look, and can be combined with a visit to the crocodile farm – Indonesia's largest – at **Pam Sunggal**.

The city is the main departure point for tours of northern Sumatra. The scenery becomes increasingly beautiful as you climb into the hills.

Lake Toba and the Toba Batak ★★

Around 3 hours from Medan and the same from Brastagi lie **Lake Toba** and **Samosir Island**, heartland of the Batak people. Like the Torajanese of Sulawesi and the Minangkabau of West Sumatra, the Bataks are proto-Malays, descendants of some of the earliest settlers of the Indonesian archipelago. They were once widely feared by their neighbours for their fierceness and their practice of ritual cannibalism. Today, although churches are packed on Sundays, animism and ancestor veneration survive.

Toba is the largest freshwater lake in Southeast Asia and, at 505m (1657ft) deep, is one of the deepest in the world. It was probably formed by a monumental volcanic eruption around 72,000 years ago. Water levels fell in the 1980s because the **Asahan River** was dammed for hydroelectricity – many large ferries can no longer dock at the Prapat ferry terminal.

The direct route to Lake Toba leads south from Medan, parallel to the coast, before turning inland for the long climb into the hills around the lake. En route, stop in **Pematangsiantar** for a visit to the **Simalungun Museum** or detour to the fortified village of **Pematang Purba**, where several tribal longhouses are preserved.

Be sure to see a *sigale-gale* puppet dance performance. These lifesize puppets were traditionally used to revive the souls of the dead, which then possessed the puppets and communicated with the living.

ACEH PROVINCE

Staunchly Islamic, Aceh has some autonomy from the government and guards its status with pride. Acehnese independence fighters were a thorn in the flesh of the Dutch and remained a thorn in the flesh of the Indonesian government, although successful peace negotiations were concluded n 2005.

Banda Aceh, the provincial capital, was one of the great world trading centres of the Middle Ages, visited by Indian, Arab, Persian, Chinese and European traders. **Kerkhof** contains the graves of more than two thousand Dutch soldiers who died in the late 1870s during Aceh wars against Dutch occupation. The Provincial Museum, on Jl Mahmudsyah, has a range of handicrafts and ceremonial clothing; the bell at the front is Chinese.

Baiturrahman Mosque (1880), the Grand Mosque, is best seen at dusk, with lights casting reflections on the lake beyond. Inside, the mosque is marble-floored and serene.

Weh Island, marking the westernmost point of Indonesia, has some of the most beautiful beaches in Sumatra, some with good diving and basic tourism facilities. Visitors should respect local customs in terms of swimwear, given local Muslim sensibilities. Banda Aceh and the west of the province will take years to recover from the tsunami, as villages are gradually rebuilt.

Above: *Orangutan mother and infant at the Bohorok Orangutan Centre.*

A USEFUL WORD

Make a friend for life by saying *Horas!* to a Batak. It means 'Hello' or 'Welcome!'

Below: *Water levels in Lake Toba have fallen in recent years, but it still retains its beauty.*

Bohorok Orangutan Centre ★

Just 2 hours from Medan, the Bohorok Orangutan Centre offers a virtually guaranteed sighting of young and mature orangutans. It lies in the jungle 40 minutes' walk along a good path from the village of Bukit Lawang. There is still a thriving, although illegal, trade in young orangutans, and most of the animals here have been rescued from it. The problem in returning the apes to the forest is that most were captured as babies. Staff teach the animals survival skills before their release into remote areas of the Gunung Leuser National Park. After a flash flood in 2003 which destroyed many of the tourist facilities the village has re-emerged as a friendly and laid-back destination popular with backpackers and domestic tourists. It's a good place to do short jungle treks.

Prapat ★★

Prapat is the main tourist base on the shore of Lake Toba, and is blissfully cool after the heat of Medan. It has wonderful views over the lake, good swimming, a Cultural Centre and a range of pleasant resort hotels. It also has a life apart from tourism: try to catch the Saturday market (near the ferry terminal), where Bataks from outlying villages come to shop, sell or just gossip.

Around Prapat

Balige, an hour or so to the south, has some interesting traditional buildings, good-quality weaving and, nearby, old tombs – many adorned with lifesize statues and carvings. **Labuhan Garaga**, about 30 minutes' drive from Prapat, is another weaving centre; the heavy cotton blankets make excellent cushion covers.

Samosir Island ★★★

Homeland of the Toba Batak, Samosir has drawn travellers for decades. The main arrival point is the traditional village of **Tomok**, which boasts the tomb of the pre-Christian Raja Sidabuta, his queen and his mistress. The small museum is worth a look. There is good shopping at stalls selling everything from carvings to musical instruments and magic calendars. The Toba Batak of Samosir are a distinct group and have several special ceremonies, including one held in July to give thanks for blessings, complete with dancing, music, traditional costumes and buffalo slaughter.

If you see no other traditional Batak village, see **Ambarita**. There are three megalithic complexes with stone seats and tables, including the flat stone slab upon which prisoners were killed.

Simanindo has a remarkable raja's palace and ancient fortifications. The 10 sets of buffalo horns on the palace each represent a generation of kings.

Brastagi and the Karo Batak

A cool hill town, Brastagi (or Berastagi) is a good base from which to explore Karo Batak villages, climb volcanoes, or sample jungle trekking and elephant rides in **Gunung Leuser National Park,** run with the participation of the local communities.

Some Karo Batak villagers live in massive clan houses raised off the ground on strong pillars and serving as home to eight or more families. People often still wear dark traditional clothes, the men in heavy black turbans and the women with broad, tasselled headdresses and huge silver earrings.

Around Brastagi

Lingga has about 30 ornately decorated clan houses. **Barusjahe** is similar to Lingga but less visited and friendlier. Ask to see the *geriten*, small replica houses, where bones of dead Karo nobles were stored. Walk on (20min) to **Sukajulu**, more for the beautiful scenery than for the village's one remaining longhouse. **Cingkes** (40min by car) has about 20 clan houses and a spirit house. **Sibolangit Botanical Gardens**, between Medan and Brastagi, has paved paths and is a good introduction to tropical vegetation.

Gunung Leuser National Park ★★

One of the largest national parks in Asia, Gunung Leuser covers more than 7750km² (3000 sq miles) and protects

---

> **EATING TIPS**
>
> If you don't like your food liberally spiced with chilli peppers, tell your waiter you want food that is *tidak pedas* – 'not spicy hot'. In Padang restaurants, waiters carry many dishes to your table balanced along their arms, and you pay only for what you eat. Many dishes are cooked in the morning and served at room temperature, with rice served hot.

Below: *Rafting through rapids on the Alas River.*

CARVINGS

Good-quality wood carvings are produced throughout Sumatra. When you get home, keep them away from direct heat – the wood may split if it dries out too quickly in centrally heated homes.

TAXIS

Many taxis in Indonesia are unmetered. Agree a price before you set off. In a metered taxi, ensure that the driver switches the meter on. If he claims that it is broken, threaten to get out of the taxi, and it will usually miraculously recover.

Below: *Known misleadingly as the Cannibal King's Dinner Table, the stone slab in Ambarita on which prisoners were put to death.*

more than 100 different mammals – including rhinoceros, tiger, elephant and orangutan – and at least 300 species of bird. The eastern fringes of the park can be visited from Brastagi, but for naturalists and trekkers the best entry point is the town of Kutacane, a half-day drive through the mountains from Brastagi.

Spectacular river-rafting trips are available down the wild Alas River through farmland and virgin rainforest; lasting 2–5 days, the adventure offers probably your best chance to see local wildlife.

Nias Island

Wild and mountainous, riven by dramatic gorges and fast-flowing rivers, Nias is an island where the culture competes with the landscape for attention. Stone staircases rise up steep mountainsides to fortified villages where the chief once sat on a stone throne, carved with writhing snakes, to watch sacrifices made on huge stone altars. In village squares 2m (6ft) high pyramidal structures were used to train young warriors to leap over protective fortifications – the origin of the ritual *fahombe* dance.

Headhunting ceased long ago and, since the arrival of Protestant missionaries, the art of megalith-building has been lost. The villages remain, however, as do the massive stone altars and megaliths. The island suffered considerable damage in the 2004 tsunami and a major earthquake a few months later. Facilities are gradually being rebuilt with the help of aid agencies.

Around Nias

Most visitors stay in beautiful **Lagundri Bay**, to the south of the island, famous for its world-class surfing, or in the small port of **Telukdalam**. The airport (served by flights from Padang and Medan) is in the north of the island at **Gunung Sitoli**.

Bawomataluwo (20min from Telukdalam) is a picture-postcard village with a huge royal palace built on piles – each one an entire treetrunk. Inside the palace are amazing carvings; the village square has further carvings and almost 300 megaliths. The village has been proposed as a World Heritage Site. Down the hill (take the stone steps) is the village of **Orahili**.

At **Hilisimaetano** around 140 traditional houses survive, as do many megaliths; stone-jumping takes place most Saturdays. **Hilimaeta**, near Lagundri (a 40min walk), has monuments including stone tables and chairs and a 2m (6ft) stone penis. Walk up to the village by a stone staircase.

WEST SUMATRA
Padang

The capital of West Sumatra province, Padang is a prosperous city and major port.

Adityawarman Museum (closed on Mondays) is built in traditional Minang style, with rice barns at the front. **Taman Budaya** (opposite the museum) is an arts institute which often stages Minang dance and *pencak silat* (martial arts) performances. Chinese temples by the small harbour, **Muara**, are symphonies of colour in red lacquer and gold leaf. **Air Manis**, a fishing village beyond Muara, is worth the 40min walk, which takes you past old Japanese cannon and a Chinese cemetery.

Around and from Padang

Bungus Bay, a 30min drive to the south, has a white sand beach and palm trees – and, unfortunately, a plywood factory. The **Solok** area, up in the mountains, is famous for its many Minang houses, rice and traditional clothes – including women's headdresses like Viking helmets consisting of lenghts of folded cloth.

If you drive to Bukittinggi, take the long route via Solok, **Lake Singkarak** and **Sulit Air** (many ravishing traditional houses). Just south of **Pariaman** a Tabut Festival is held each year (usually in August): villagers build and decorate *bouraq* – winged horses with the face of a woman – which are paraded through the streets, with mock fights ensuing whenever two *bouraq* cross paths.

EAST-COAST ATTRACTIONS

Independence Day (Aug 17) celebrations in **Palembang** include the **Bidar Race** on the Musi River; long, narrow canoes shaped like animals powered by up to 50 oarsmen. The city's **Rumah Bari Museum** has mesolithic sculptures from the Pasemah Highlands and a 200-year-old royal barge. **Candi Muara Takus** is a Buddhist stupa complex thought to date from the 9th century. **Siak Palace**, 2 hours from Pekanbaru, is an amazing Moorish-style building (built in 1889), all columns and chandeliers. There are more ancient temple remains at the Muara Jambi complex an hour's drive or boat trip from the city.

Below: *Near Bukittinggi, a village on the shore of Maninjau crater lake.*

Below: *A coconut collector in West Sumatra: the macaque climbs the trees for him.*

Minangkabau Highlands

High above the steaming coastal heat of Padang lies **Bukittinggi**, capital of the Minangkabau people. This area draws thousands of visitors every year, with foreign tourists increasingly joined by domestic tourists from Java. The attraction is the beautiful mountain scenery combined with a fascinating culture and pleasant climate. Anthropologists, too, continue to be drawn to the Minangkabau Highlands by a culture which is both Muslim and matriarchal.

Bukittinggi

The name means 'high hill', and the town is stunningly located with views over fertile valleys to two volcanoes, **Mt Merapi** and **Mt Singgalang**. Although Merapi has not erupted seriously since the 1980s, puffs of smoke and occasionally small ash explosions can be seen from across the valley, and it is best to check locally if the mountain is considered safe.

The town itself is clean, relaxed and prosperous. It is a tradition for young men to journey to other parts of Indonesia to seek their fortune before returning home to get married, and the Minang are respected across Indonesia for their sharp business sense. Bukittinggi is laid out in tiers down the steep hillside, each level connected to the next by precipitous stone steps and passageways.

Your first port of call should be the aptly named **Panorama Park**, which has spectacular views over the Sianok and Ngarai canyons. Stairs take you down to the valley bottom for the two-hour walk to the silver-smithing centre of **Koto Gedang**.

Below the town square, with its old Dutch clock tower, is a colourful market that draws villagers from far around, with stalls selling everything from chilli peppers to love potions.

Bukittinggi's zoo offers a chance to see many different animals and birds in a beautiful parkland setting. Below the zoo are caves excavated by the Japanese during World War II and now promoted as a tourist attraction. Far more spectacular – although further afield (25 minutes by car) – is the **Ngalau Kamang cave complex**, with spectacular stalactites and stalagmites.

From Bukittinggi

A 30min drive through rich river valleys with multidomed mosques and tantalizing glimpses of traditional Minang houses takes you to **Padangpanjang**, famous for its rain, its cold nights and its musical conservatory, **ASKI**. Live performances of traditional Minangkabau dance and music, as well as *gamelan*, feature during term-times, which approximate to those of the European academic year.

Some 40 minutes west of Bukittinggi, through lush, rolling hills, lies the huge and beautiful crater lake of **Maninjau**. Walk down from the top of the hill (about an hour) to get the full enjoyment of the peace and the views.

At **Batusankar** you can see the splendidly restored palace, with its wonderful carved and painted façades. Even at weekends, when there are crowds, it is intensely atmospheric. **Balimbing** village has many traditional Minang homes.

Harau Canyon, near Payakumbuh, is a deep canyon with a beautiful waterfall (best at the end of the rainy season) and many butterflies; avoid weekends, when it becomes very crowded. Steam-train buffs must see **Padangpanjang Station**, where relics rust stylishly in sidings. Giant rafflesia flowers are sometimes found at a sanctuary at **Batang Palapuh**, near Lake Maninjau.

Below: *Typical Minang-kabau architecture in the splendid setting of the Harau Canyon.*

Kerinci Seblat National Park ★★

A 7-hour drive from Padang, the 14,000km² (5404 sq mile) Kerinci Seblat is one of the most important wildlife parks in Southeast Asia. In 1998 an ambitious US$25 million World Bank project was launched to safeguard it against a range of threats. Endangered animals include Sumatran tigers, clouded leopard, tapir, rhinoceroses and elephant – but no orangutans (on Sumatra these occur only north of Lake Toba). Local people and researchers continue to report seeing something even stranger: an apelike creature known as orang pendek (short man). It has not yet been accepted by science, but there is mounting evidence as to its existence.

The focal point of the park is the active volcano Mt Kerinci, at 3800m (12,500ft) the highest mountain in Indonesia outside Papua. Most visitors base themselves in the small market town of **Sungeipenuh**, in the densely populated river valley. The town is a 20min drive from **Lake Kerinci**, which offers beautiful and easy walking to villages around the lakeshore.

The 2-hour drive from Sungeipenuh to Mt Kerinci is by a good road and offers superlative views. The climb up the mountain takes two days – be prepared for a cold night camping out on the slopes. At the base of **Mt Tujuh**, near Palompek village below Mt Kerinci, is a National Park forest guesthouse. Climb on via jungle trails to **Lake Tujuh** (3 hours), an eerily beautiful crater lake. An hour from the guesthouse is the enormous **Letter W Waterfall**.

Bengkulu

A university town and administrative centre, Bengkulu was the last territory in Indonesia to be held by the British. The British presence was established in 1685, but the city's fame and prosperity reached its apogee in the early 19th century under Sir Thomas Stamford Raffles, who went on to found Singapore. Today Bengkulu is a pleasant city on the shores of the Indian Ocean with many tree-lined roads and small parks.

Fort Marlborough dates from 1714. Nearby is the **British Governor's mansion**, its classical façade overrun by vines and banyan-tree roots. The **Kuburan**

Below: *Mount Kerinci broods over Kerinci Seblat.*

Belanda ('foreigners' Graveyard') dates back to the early 18th century and illustrates how fragile life could be in the tropics at that time. **Pantai Panjang** ('Long Beach') stretches for kilometres. Be careful – the surf produces strong undertows.

Around Bengkulu

Tabah Penanjung, an hour into the hills above Bengkulu, is a nature reserve where rafflesia are often found. **Mt Bukit Kaba**, near the pleasant hill town of Curup, can be climbed in a day from Bengkulu if you leave early; the mountain boasts three immense craters and bubbling sulphur fountains. South of Bengkulu, the coastline is beautiful on the way to the little town of **Krui.** Stay at **Krui** or **Liwa** to explore the Bukit Barisan National Park, which is included in the Global 200 Ecoregions, WWF's ranking of the world's most biologically outstanding habitats.

Lampung

At the extreme south of Sumatra, Lampung province is overlooked by most tourists. In the past it was well known for its marvellous 'ship cloths', some using real gold thread, and for its pepper; in the 1970s and 80s it was the location for ambitious transmigration projects, resettling farmers from overpopulated Java. It boasts volcanoes, wildlife reserves, megalithic remains and a superb coastline of deep-cut bays and wonderful beaches.

The provincial capital is **Bandar Lampung**, made up of the twin cities of Telukbetung and Tanjungkarang. The area was devastated by tsunamis generated by the 1883 eruption of **Krakatau**, and in Telukbetung a ship's buoy lies where it was thrown, halfway up a hill. In Bandar Lampung, visit the provincial museum at Jl Teuku Umar for archaeological exhibits and exquisite antique fabrics.

Way Kambas National Park is a 130,000ha (320,000-acre) area of freshwater swamp and lowland forest with wild elephant, tapir and many other animals, including a good range of birds. The first elephant trainiing centre in Indonesia started here in the mid-1980s, since when it has attempted to deal with some of Sumatra's surplus elephants by domesticating them and sending them to zoos and safari parks.

Sumatra's East Coast

After the mountains and rainforests of West Sumatra, the flatness of the east coast is a shock. This is a land of big skies and oil rigs and nights lit by natural-gas flares: the area is the major source of Indonesia's oil and gas wealth. Giant rivers like the **Musi** and **Siak** snake their way from sources more than 150km (100 miles) inland through mangrove swamps and jungle, past settlements on stilts, to ports like Pekanbaru, midway up the coast, and Palembang, which has historical records going back 13 centuries. The islands of **Batam** and **Bintan** are part of the Southeast Asian '**golden triangle**' of economic growth, with industries and tourist resorts, including luxury hotels and golf courses which cater largely to the weekend Singapore market.

Sumatra at a Glance

GETTING THERE

By air: Major cities in Sumatra have regular flights to Jakarta and, in the case of Medan, to Singapore and Penang in Malaysia.

By sea: For those with more time to spare, the state shipping company Pelni runs efficient passenger ships linking the main ports (including Medan and Padang). Travel first-class for comfort.

GETTING AROUND

Road travel is no longer the ordeal it was, and roads are improving every year. But don't underestimate the distances involved. Cars with drivers and guides are easily organized in all main centres.

WHERE TO STAY

The main centres – Medan, Banda Aceh, Padang, Bukittinggi, Brastagi, Lake Toba, etc. – have a good range of international hotels. Elsewhere, be prepared to compromise.

Banda Aceh
LUXURY

Hermes Palace Hotel, Jl Panglima Nyak Makam, tel: (0651) 755 5888, fax: (0651) 755 5999, www. hermespalace.com

Medan
LUXURY

Tiara Medan, Kl Cut Mutiah, tel: (061) 457 4000, fax: (061) 451 0176, www. tiara-hotel.com

Polonia, Jl Sudirmand 14–18, tel: (061) 414 2222, fax: (061) 453 8870, www.hotelpolonia.com
Hotel Sahid Medan, Jl Sisingamangaraja 11, Km 7.5, tel: (061) 787 9070, fax: (021) 787 9147, www.sahid.com

MID-RANGE

Hotel Danau Toba, Jl Imam Bonjol 17, tel: (061) 415 7000, fax: (061) 453 0553, www.hoteldanautoba.com
Garuda Plaza, Jl Sisingamangaraja 18, tel: (061) 736 1234, fax: (061) 736 1111, www.garudahotel.com
Novotel Seochi, Jl Cirebon 76a, tel: (061) 456 1234, fax: (061) 457 2222.

Brastagi

There is a wide choice of accommodation including the resort hotel **Sibayak Internasional**, Jl Merdeka, tel: (0628) 91301, fax: (0628) 91307, www.hotelsibayak.com
Berastagi Cottages, Jl Gundaling, tel: (0628) 720421, fax: (0628) 717522; pleasant, well out of town, excellent food.

Prapat

Dozens of hotels and guesthouses to choose from, although weekends can get busy. Among the nicest are:
Natour Hotel Prapat, Jl Marihat 1, tel: (0625) 41012, fax: (0625) 41019; pleasant old Dutch-style hotel with modern additions.
Danau Toba Internasional, Jl Pulau Samosir 17, tel: (0625) 41583, fax: (0625) 41119; well located, very comfortable.

Samosir Island

Accommodation on Samosir is directed mainly towards visitors wanting to forget the 21st century for a few days. Most of the accommodation is simple, although some more comfortable hotels have been developed. The main places to stay are Tuk Tuk and Ambarita.

Tuk Tuk

Dozens of guesthouses serve the young backpackers. The famed **Carolina Cottages**, tel: (0625) 41520, has a lakeside location and good tourist services. Alternatives are the **Bagus Bay Homestay**, tel: (0625) 451287, and the more upmarket **Tabo Cottages**, tel: (0625) 451318, fax: (0625) 451614, www.tabocottages.com

Ambarita

Barbara's, tel: (0625) 41230, has a well-established reputation for friendliness, while the **Sopo Toba**, tel: (0625) 41616, is more of a traditional resort hotel, and one of the most upmarket on the island. Located about 6km (nearly 4 miles) from Ambarita is the **Shangri-La**, tel: (0625) 41724, a comfortable hotel with good service.

Nias

There are several basic guesthouses around Lagundri Bay and Sorake Beach aimed at backpackers and surfers, with facilities to match. More upmarket is the **Sorake Beach Resort**, Lagundri Bay, tel: (0630) 21195.

Sumatra at a Glance

Padang
Hotel Bumiminang, Jl Bundo
Kandung 20–28, tel: (0751)
37555, fax: (0751) 37567,
www.bumiminang.com
Pangeran Beach Hotel,
Jl Ir H. Juanda 79, tel: (0751)
31333, fax: (0751) 54613.
Natour Muara, Jl Gereja 34, tel:
(0751) 35600, fax: (0751) 31613.
Hotel Dipo International, Jl
Diponegoro 13, tel: (0751)
34261.

Bukittinggi
As this is a popular backpacker
destination, many guesthouses
at the lower end of the market
sprang up, followed by more
upmarket hotels, such as:
Pusako, Jl Soekarno-Hatta 7, tel:
(0752) 32111, fax: (0752) 32667.
Novotel, Jl Laras Datuk
Bandaro, tel: (0752) 35000,
fax: (0752) 23800,
www.novotelbukittinggi.com
Denai, Jl Dr Rivai 26, tel: (0752)
32920, fax: (0752) 33490. This
is smaller and very pleasant.

Sungaipenuh
All the hotels in this town
are basic. Amongst the more
comfortable are the **Hotel
Aroma**, tel: (0748) 21142, in
the town centre; the **Hotel
Busana**, tel: (0748) 21122; and
the **Masgo**, tel: (0748) 323603.

Bengkulu
Horison, Jl Pantai Nala 142, tel:
(0736) 21722, fax: (0736) 22072.
Nala Beach Cottages, Jl Pantai
Nala 133, tel/fax: (0736)
21855; this has nice cottages
and good views.

Bandar Lampung
Most hotels in this area
can help visitors to
organize trips to Way
Kambas (around two hours
from the city). These trips
generally include boat trips
up the Way Kanan River.
Sahid Bandar Lampung,
Jl Yos Sudarso 294,
tel: (0721) 488888,
fax: (0751) 486589.
Sheraton Lampung Hotel,
Jl Walter Monginsidi 175,
tel: (0721) 486666,
fax: (0721) 486690.
Marcopolo, Jl Dr Susilo 4,
tel: (0721) 262511,
fax: (0721) 254419.

Palembang
Sanjaya, Jl Kapten A. Rivai
6193, tel: (0711) 310675,
fax: (0711) 313693
–Palembang's finest.
Hotel King's, Kol. Atmo 623,
tel: (0711) 36232, fax: (0711)
310937.

Pekanbaru
Sri Indrayani, Jl Dr Sam
Ratulangi, tel: (0761) 35600,
fax: (0761) 31870.
Mutiara Merdeka, Jl Yos
Sudarso 12, tel: (0761) 31272,
fax: (0761) 32959.

Medan
Jl Achmad Yani, the city's main
shopping street for souvenirs,
has dozens of shops selling
Batak carvings, fabrics and
other tribal artefacts. The huge
Medan Mall has clothing shops
and good food outlets.

Padang
For souvenirs and artefacts
Bukittinggi is probably better,
but the **Matahari Shopping
Centre** (Jl Moh Yamin) has
clothing and basic necessities,
while **Sartika** (Jl Sudirman 5)
has souvenirs.

Bengkulu
Goldsmiths in **Kampung Cina**,
near Fort Marlborough, work
with locally mined gold, while
the local speciality textile is
called batik besurek, which –
unusually for Indonesian textiles
– has the pattern hand-painted
on after weaving.

Bandar Lampung
Traditional tapis sarongs are
now museum pieces. Shops sell
less ornate but good-quality fabrics. Try **Putra Indonesia** (Jl S
Parman 37) or **Batik Indonesia**
(Jl Dwi Warna 1).

MEDAN	J	F	M	A	M	J	J	A	S	O	N	D
AVERAGE TEMP. °F	80	80	80	80	80	80	80	80	78	78	78	78
AVERAGE TEMP. °C	27	27	27	27	27	27	27	27	26	26	26	26
HOURS OF SUN DAILY	5	7	6	6	6	7	7	6	4	4	5	4
RAINFALL in	4	4	6	7	10	6	7	7	11	11	9	10
RAINFALL mm	92	108	158	187	248	161	188	171	277	229	229	245
DAYS OF RAINFALL	14	10	15	16	20	14	17	17	23	19	19	19

3
Kalimantan

Land of the **Dayaks** – a collective name for more than 200 tribes – and of vast, ancient rainforests, Kalimantan (the Indonesian part of Borneo) draws the adventurous today as it has for centuries. Many are brought here by the wildlife, the white-water rapids and the untracked depths of the jungle. But for many others the greatest lure is the Dayak people.

A DIVIDED LAND

Providing Indonesia with its longest land-border, the island of Borneo is governed by three separate nations: tiny Brunei Darussalam and the Malaysian states of Sarawak and Sabah in the north, while the lower two-thirds belong to Indonesia. This division was settled by an Anglo-Dutch treaty in 1824, but gave rise to military clashes in 1963 between Sukarno's turbulent Indonesia and the newly-independent Malaysia, backed by Britain.

The most striking feature of the Dayak cultures is their social organisation, with dozens of families traditionally living in the same building, which can be up to 500 metres (500 yards) long. Each family has its own compartments within the house. People live by agriculture and by hunting: many men are still amazingly skilled with the blowpipe, although spears are more common.

Travel anywhere in Kalimantan in the old days was by water, and even nowadays the rivers – massive and slow-flowing as they near the sea, turbulent and fast in the upper reaches – are still important arteries of communication. More often, though, small aeroplanes link remote settlements,

Opposite: *Banjarmasin's floating Kuin Market, on the Barito River.*

DON'T MISS

***Mahakam River**: enjoy an enchanting journey by river bus or houseboat.
Banjarmasin: buy precious stones – diamonds, emeralds and sapphires – at bargain prices.
*Loksado and the Meratus Mountains**: easy treks lead into the hills of South Kalimantan to visit traditional villages.

TREASURES FOR SALE

Beautifully woven rattan baskets, *mandau* (Dayak machetes), and painted war shields make great souvenirs, either from the villages or from Samarinda. Backpack-style baby-carriers are fantastically decorated with beading, bear teeth and claws and wild boar tusks, but genuine ones are rare.

ERAU FESTIVAL

The Erau festival is held in Tenggarong in September, usually in the last week of the month. Dayak tribes from all over East Kalimantan arrive for this three-day cultural festival with dancing, rituals, song and canoe races which celebrates the founding of the town. Unmissable.

landing on rough grassy strips cleared from the forest.

Headhunting was practised by some of the tribal groups in the past, with various ritual beliefs associated with the practice. For instance, taking a 'strong' head could guarantee a successful rice harvest and protect a longhouse against disease and other headhunters, and was essential for marriage and funeral ceremonies. Headhunting was eradicated by the joint actions of missionaries and Dutch administrators before World War II, and today young Dayak men leave the longhouse to prove their manhood in the sawmills and oil fields of the coast, sending back televisions and other consumer goods rather than severed heads.

EAST KALIMANTAN – GATEWAY TO THE DAYAKS

Don't expect to see jungles and tattooed Dayak warriors as soon as you arrive at Balikpapan or Samarinda. Decades of logging and forest fires have left scrappy, infertile land cultivated in patches by a few Javanese settlers.

Balikpapan and Surrounds

The main arrival point for most visitors to East Kalimantan is Balikpapan, a wealthy oil city and port. Most visitors then move on to Samarinda – ideally by boat up the coast, but otherwise by road through a deforested landscape with the occasional distant glimpse of rainforest.

The old sultanate of **Pasir Belengkong** is a long day's excursion from Balikpapan by hired car and river bus. Go first to the small market town of **Tanahgrogot** and then take a river bus upstream to Belengkong, past sago-palm swamps and stilted houses. The village has a rambling old palace, wood carvings, and collections of antique china and cannon.

Samarinda

It is a 2–3-hour drive to Samarinda from Balikpapan. Alternatively, take a taxi to **Pasar Baru** and then a speedboat along the coast and upriver to Samarinda. Wrap up well and protect your camera from the spray.

While Balikpapan is founded on oil wealth, Samarinda is East Kalimantan's timber town. The city is cut neatly in half by the mighty **Mahakam River**. Ocean-going freighters travel more than 50km (30 miles) inland to dock within metres of the city's great white-domed mosque, and huge rafts of forest timbers float on the mud-brown waters of the river, awaiting their turn at the city's sawmills.

Young girls weave intricate sarongs, famous across Indonesia, and 'art shops' sell old and new Dayak carvings and antique china. The city is intensely hot, humid and rather grubby, but it has a distinctive style of its own, particularly for those wishing to emulate a character in a Joseph Conrad novel.

From Samarinda you can, via the Mahakam, embark on epic sorties deep into the interior – or simply take a 2-hour boat ride upriver to **Tenggarong**, capital of the old **Kutai Regency**. The **Sultan's Palace** there has been converted into a superb museum with stunning Dayak carvings and wonderful ceramics.

The Mahakam River ★★★

There are trips for all budgets. The most comfortable way is to charter a houseboat, while the young and hardy take to the river in a river-bus packed with homeward-bound Dayaks, incontinent goats and smelly hunt-

BOAR HUNTING

The majority of the Dayak of inland East Kalimantan are Christian, and wild boar plays an important part in their diet. A day out hunting is a memorable experience. The hunters use spears and dogs, the latter flushing out the pig and holding it at bay until the hunters arrive. Blowpipes are mainly used by the semi-nomadic Penan of the north.

Below: *The silhouette of this tract of rainforest near Samarinda is ragged, betraying that the area has been logged.*

Above: *Travelling by boat through the Tanjung Puting National Park allows close-up views of the rainforest.*

ing dogs. Either way, the trip will be memorable. However, there are no rainforest giants festooned with orchids or some of Kalimantan's 1100 different fern species along the river banks: the chainsaws came here long ago, and you must travel deep inland to see true virgin forest.

From Tenggarong the river winds inland through swampy lowlands to the small town of **Muara Muntai**, the last major settlement before you enter the complex of shallow lakes that offer your best chance to see the rare freshwater dolphin of the Mahakam. By the time you get here, the forest is thicker.

Most visitors detour by motorized canoe across shallow **Lake Jempang** to the Benuaq village of **Tanjung Isuy**, where traditional dance performances are regularly staged. The old, carved longhouse has been turned into a guesthouse. Double back to Muara Muntai and then continue upriver to **Melak**, from where jeeps take visitors to the orchid reserve of **Kersik Luwai**. The orchids bloom towards the end of the rainy season, in March or April.

Most tour groups do no more than pay a fleeting visit to this area before heading back to Samarinda or Balikpapan, yet the villages around Melak – and especially around **Barong Tongkok** – are fascinating. Though Melak is the last port of call for most organized trips, the river of course goes on … and so do adventurous travellers with time to spare.

SOUTH AND CENTRAL KALIMANTAN

Known as the **Land of a Thousand Rivers**, this area has neither the dramatic mountain scenery nor the cultural attractions of East Kalimantan – although there are inland Dayak tribes and traditional villages. It does, however, boast one of Kalimantan's more interesting cities – **Banjarmasin** – as well as diamond mining on inland rivers (notably around Cempaka and Martapura), and the **Tanjung Puting National Park**, base for the orangutan study centre at **Camp Leakey**.

Banjarmasin ★

Lying on the delta of the massive **Barito River**, Banjarmasin is a staunchly Islamic trading city which seems completely at ease with its watery surroundings. Many of the older houses are actually rafts, rising and falling with the tide, while the entire city is crisscrossed with canals and creeks. Enjoy the fabulous sunsets which can dye the peat-heavy waters of the Barito, with its floating mats of water-hyacinth, the colour of blood.

The city acts as a clearing house for the diamond-mining operations of the interior. If you know your stones – and if you are careful – you can buy cut and uncut diamonds, emeralds and sapphires at prices so low you could fund your entire trip from the profits.

Tamban is approximately 20 minutes upriver from the city centre and is one of Banjarmasin's 'floating cities'. Thousands of wooden houses constructed on floats are connected by wooden walkways and fairly evil-smelling canals. **Kuin Market**, not far from **Trisakti Harbour**, is the largest of Banjar's colourful floating markets, but you have to get there early in the morning: it is virtually over by 08:30. Gorge yourself on sweet, sticky cakes from the floating cafés.

Martapura and Cempaka ★★

An easy day trip from Banjarmasin, these two towns are the centre of diamond mining in South Kalimantan. In **Martapura**, make a point of visiting the town market and nearby diamond-polishing factory.

The Meratus Mountains ★

This group of hills forms the spine of South Kalimantan, and they are still dotted with the traditional villages of the Bukit group of Dayaks. Treks lasting anything from a day upwards start from Loksado (4 hours from Banjarmasin), from where you can also make an exciting trip along the Amandit River on bamboo rafts – expect to get wet!

Palangkaraya

This sprawling settlement, on the banks of the Kahayan river, is the provincial capital of Central Kalimantan. It holds an annual cultural festival in May, the Isen Mulang, which celebrates Dayak arts such as canoe-racing and blow-pipes.

THE INTERIOR

For a foray into the true heartland of Kalimantan, fly in via the jungle airstrip near the Kenyah Dayak village of **Long Ampung**. This is the access point for the magnificent mountains and virgin rainforests of the **Apo Kayan** region. Unless you speak Indonesian, bring a guide with you from Samarinda.

From Samarinda, a road leads north to the little-visited **Kutai National Park**, which still has populations of orangutans and proboscis monkeys despite fires and illegal logging in recent decades. Trips to Kutai can be organized from Samarinda or Balikpapan, or hotels in Bontang can help provide guides. Kutai Guesthouse, in the park itself, has helpful staff.

Another excursion is to fly up the coast to Tarakan near the Malaysian border, then double back to explore the villages of the **Berau Regency** and the **Krayan Delta**. The islands off the coast, centering on **Derawan**, comprise a marine reserve; their beaches are used by nesting sea turtles, and there are some fine coral reefs. The Derawan Dive Resort has good dive facilities. Contact www.divederawan.com

---

Opposite bottom: *A longhouse converted for visitors at Tanjung Isuy using traditional styles and materials.*

Above: *Feeding time for the orangutans at the Tanjung Puting National Park's Camp Leakey.*

TRIPS INTO THE INTERIOR

Organized trips into the interior of Kalimantan are available through Samarinda and Balikpapan tour operators who have links with agents in Jakarta, Bali and overseas. Be warned, though: such expeditions can be expensive, and should be booked only via a specialist operator.

KAHARINGAN

Many Dayak were converted to Christianity or Islam, but adherence to the traditional religion – kaharingan – is strong. The government classifies the religion as Hinduism. Many ritual practices are shamanistic, with priests entering a trance and acting as an intermediary to restore harmony between the world of mortals and the spirit world.

Tanjung Puting National Park ★

The major draw here is **Camp Leakey**, an orangutan centre two hours upstream from Kumai. The orangutans are well acclimatized to the presence of human beings. A huge area of lowland peat forest and swamp, the park is rich in a variety of other animals too, including crocodiles, otters, sun-bears, gibbons and the entertaining proboscis monkeys. The magnificent birdlife is best seen from a dugout canoe; these can be hired from the well-appointed **Rimba Lodge**, which can only be accessed by river-boat.

WEST KALIMANTAN

For years West Kalimantan has been of little interest to foreign visitors, but it is now a useful entry or exit point for Indonesia with good land connections to Kuching, in the Malaysian state of Sarawak. It also has an embryonic tourist industry based on the national parks of **Gunung Palung** and **Bentuang Karimun**. Perhaps more than almost anywhere else in Indonesia, visitors will need fortitude, an adventurous spirit and a reasonable command of Bahasa Indonesia to overcome the challenges of travelling here, since the tourist infrastructure is practically non-existent.

Pontianak

Famous for its sunsets, the provincial capital, Pontianak, is an unpretentious city, bustling with floating markets and canals. The main sights are the **Istana Kadriyah**, the old royal palace, built of ironwood in 1771, and still inhabited by descendants of the royal family, and the **Abdurrakhman Mosque**, with its Javanese-style roof. A monument marks the city's location on the Equator. A stroll along the waterfront offers pleasantly bustling scenes, but expect to be mobbed by children wanting their photographs taken. **Pinisi Harbour** has lots of Buginese and Javanese schooners, together with huge houseboats which act as floating shops trading up and down the **Kapuas River**.

Pontianak National Museum, built in traditional style, has a good selection of West Kalimantan Dayak costumes and crafts, ceramics and musical instruments. A complete longhouse (known locally as a *betang*) stands in the grounds.

Fly direct from Surabaya, Jakarta or Sulawesi to Pontianak, Balikpapan or Banjarmasin. Also flights from Singapore and Kuching (Sarawak) to Pontianak and from Singapore to Balikpapan.

A sparse network of roads connects the major coastal cities, but distances are huge and long journeys are best made by air. Inland, transport is either by small aircraft, or increasingly by bus or chartered vehicle rather than boat as the road network expands. Away from the roads, revert to the rivers – or walk.

Balikpapan
Hotel Altea Benakutai, Jl P Antasari, tel: (0542) 35896, fax: (0542) 31823.
Hotel Blue Sky, Jl Letjen Suprapto, tel: (0542) 35895, fax: (0542) 24094, www.blueskybalikpapan.com
Dusit Balikpapan, Jl Jend Sudirman, tel: (0542) 420 155, fax: (0542) 420 150.

Samarinda
Mesra International, Jl Pahlawan 1, tel: (0541) 732 772, fax: (0541) 735 453.
Bumi Senyiur Hotel, Jl Diponegoro 17-19, tel: (0541) 735 101, fax: (0541) 738 014, www.bumi.senyiur.hotels.com

Bontang
The **Cahaya Bone Hotel**, Jl Par-

man Km 6, tel: (0548) 22798, can help organize guides to the Kutai National Park.

Banjarmasin
Arum Kalimantan, Jl Lambung Mangkurat, tel: (0511) 66818, fax: (0511) 67345.
Swiss-Belhotel Borneo, Jl Pangeran Antasari 86A, tel: (0511) 327 1111, www.swiss-belhotel.com
Tanjung Puting National Park, Rimba Lodge, tel: (0532_671 0589, fax: (0532) 21923, www.rimbalodge.com

Pontianak
Mahkota Hotel, Jl Sidas 8, tel: (0561) 36022, fax: (0561) 36200, www.grandmahkotahotel.com
Kapuas Palace Hotel, Jl Imam Bonjol, tel: (0561) 36122, fax: (0561) 34374.
Kartika Hotel, Jl Rahadi Usman, tel: (0561) 34401, fax: (0561) 38457. Small business-class hotel.

Balikpapan
Look for Dayak handicrafts, woven rattan basketry, *mandau* machetes, Punan blowpipes, carvings and

some genuinely old ceramics. **Syadah Mestika**, at Jl Yani 2, is a good outlet.

Samarinda
Again good for Dayak crafts, although some beadwork items are made by entrepreneurial individuals in the town rather than upriver in the longhouses as tourists fondly imagine. Serious collectors can pick up excellent 'primitive' carvings. If you know ceramics, you may still find 17th- and 18th-century porcelain and Ming, Sung and Khmer funerary ware (but some items are stolen from graves).

Banjarmasin
Gems, gems and more gems – with Dayak handicrafts and local tie-dyed textiles called *sasirangan* thrown in for good measure. There are craft and souvenir centres on Jl Sudimampir, along with gem dealers; **Ida**, in particular, is worth a visit – there are some fantastic Ming pieces along with Delft china and old Banjar brassware.

Pontianak
Look for ceramics, Dayak work and hand-woven silks.

PONTIANAK	J	F	M	A	M	J	J	A	S	O	N	D
AVERAGE TEMP. °F	78	78	80	80	82	82	82	82	80	80	80	80
AVERAGE TEMP. °C	26	26	27	27	28	28	28	28	27	27	27	27
HOURS OF SUN DAILY	4	4	4	5	6	6	6	6	5	5	5	4
RAINFALL in	27	20	13	11	10	8	8	8	10	13	14	18
RAINFALL mm	683	522	330	286	253	199	199	211	271	326	343	465
DAYS OF RAINFALL	18	17	16	22	23	16	20	17	28	30	24	27

4
Java

Java is an island of great natural beauty, despite the challenges posed by the high population. Family-planning campaigns have had an effect, and the fertility of the soil, diversity of manufacturing, and industriousness of the people ensure a rising standard of living. With its scenery of volcanoes, rice-fields and traditional villages, much of the landscape is still rural. In **West Java**, the ancient kingdom of **Sunda**, there is superlative wild scenery, some of it protected by wildlife reserves. **East Java** has peaceful hill towns where time seems, if not to stand still, then at least to slow down. And **Central Java** is a fantastic landscape of dramatic volcanoes and river valleys, with clay-roofed hamlets surrounded by groves of fruit trees.

JAKARTA

Capital of one of the world's fastest-growing economies, Jakarta has over twelve million people – and is expanding almost by the minute. Traffic and air pollution can be ghastly, and the heat and humidity sap your strength. The key to enjoying the city is not to fight its pace and size, its heat, humidity and crowds, but to accept them. It's worth it, for the city has plenty to offer.

Laid out on a north–south axis, Jakarta boasts some of the finest museums in Asia, the remarkable **Taman Mini cultural park**, a fascinating old town (**Kota**) and huge contrasts between the brash new buildings of the main streets and the older residential areas behind them.

CLIMATE

Java can be visited at any time of year, although it is slightly cooler and less humid during the months of June to August. The heaviest rains are normally from December to March). East Java has a drier climate than West Java. Temperatures quickly drop with altitude.

Opposite: *An eruption of Mt Semeru, with the crater of Mt Bromo in the foreground.*

DON'T MISS

★★★ Bogor Botanical Gardens: luxuriant tropical vegetation and knowledge-able guides.

★★★ Krakatau: possibly the world's most famous volcano.

★★★ Ujung Kulon National Park: primary rainforest where leopards and the last Javan rhinos thrive.

★★★ Taman Sari: Yogyakarta's exquisite Water Palace.

★★★ Candi Lorojonggrang: a vast, spectacular Hindu temple at Prambanan, cur-rently being rebuilt after the 2006 earthquake.

★★★ Borobudur: The largest Buddhist temple in the world and a World Heritage Site.

★★★ Mt Bromo: a panorama of volcanoes and lava flows.

★★ Taman Mini: A good introduction to the rich cul-tural heritage of the archipel-ago, with architecture and artefacts from all over.

★★ Surabaya Post Office: An impressive Art Deco building with wonderful attention to detail.

Kota (Old Batavia) ★★★

In the north of the city, this is the oldest and most atmos-pheric part of Jakarta. Here are some of the best museums in Indonesia alongside wonderful old buildings. Aim to spend a full day in Kota, arriving very early to enjoy the cooler part of the day. Start exploring at **Sunda Kelapa**, where hundreds of wooden Buginese ships moor. From the harbour, walk through the lively **Pasar Ikan** ('Fish Market') area to **Museum Bahari**, a well-laid-out maritime museum in two 17th-century Dutch warehouses. En route, look at the Baroque interior of **Gereja Sion**, Jakarta's oldest church (1695).

Continue to **Taman Fatahillah**, once the main city square of Batavia. The cannon in the square (**Si Jagur**) is almost worn smooth by the embraces of local women who believe touching it cures infertility. On one side of the square, in a classical colonnaded building, is the **Balai Seni Rupa (Museum of Fine Arts)**, with some good paintings and carvings. The smaller **Ceramic Museum** in the same building is even better. Cross the square to the beautifully restored 18th-century Dutch **Stadhuis**, now housing the **Old Batavia Museum (Museum Kota)**. Underground are the grim water dungeons where condemned men lay in cells flooded daily by the Ciliwung River. Just beyond, on Jl Pintu Besar Utara, is the fascinating **Wayang Museum**, with puppets and costumes from all over Indonesia.

An enjoyable way to tour the Kota sights is to charter a *becak* (cycle-taxi) for the day. The driver will wait for you at each of the museums. Between visits, take some refreshment at the magnificent Art Deco Café Batavia – not cheap, but well worth the outlay for the ambience!

OUT OF THE CENTRE
Taman Mini ★★
An overview of Indonesia's myriad cultures can be found at the Taman Mini cultural theme park, 30 minutes by car from central Jakarta. The park, complete with cable car and a huge lake, has exhibitions of arts, architecture and crafts from all of Indonesia's provinces. Inside a giant Komodo dragon is a wildlife museum; the **Indonesia Museum** is equally fascinating. A short walk takes you to a huge bird park with several aviaries.

Above: *A Dutch colonial building in the Kota district of Jakarta.*

Ragunan Zoo ★
Well worth a visit for anybody interested in Indonesian wildlife. The animals – including gibbons, Sumatran tigers, Komodo dragons and Sumatran rhinoceroses – are kept in large enclosures in a pleasant parkland environment. (The zoo becomes crowded at weekends.)

Textile Museum ★
This small museum at Jl Satsuit Tuban 4 in Tanah Abang has over 600 exhibits from all over the archipelago, including batik and sumptuous *ikat* weaving from Sumba and Flores. Definitely worth a visit if you plan to buy quality textiles later on.

NEARBY
Pulau Seribu (Thousand Islands) ★
The coral atolls of the Thousand Island group are almost as perfect in real life as they look from the air as your plane comes in to land at Jakarta airport. The beaches are white, the water is generally crystal clear and the peace is delicious. The more distant islands – **Putri**, **Pantara**, **Pelangi** and **Kotok** – have cottage-style hotels and diving facilities, with good coral reefs nearby. Transport to and accommodation on all the islands can be booked through most travel agents in Jakarta – for weekends, advance booking is essential.

MEDAN MERDEKA, JAKARTA

Get your bearings by locating Medan Merdeka. One of the largest city squares in the world, this is lined with government offices, the glowing white **Presidential Palace** and the vast **Istiqlal Mosque**. At the centre is the **National Monument (Monas)**, a 135m (450ft) gold-topped obelisk. A lift inside the tower takes you to the top for a panoramic view of Jakarta.

On the west of the square is Indonesia's **National Museum**, with a new wing opened in 2006. Anybody interested in anthropology, crafts, archaeology or Chinese ceramics could spend days in here. A few minutes away, down Jl Cikini Raya, is **Taman Ismail Marzuki (TIM)**, Jakarta's main showcase for the performing arts, with art galleries, auditoria and a sensational range of performances.

WEST JAVA

The ancient kingdom of Sunda, now the heartland of West Java, boasts wonderful mountain scenery, world-famous botanical gardens and national parks sucj as **Ujung Kulon**, **Gunung Halimun** and **Gunung Gede-Pangrango**, which protect some finds stands of tropical rainforest. But the long-gone rulers of Sunda built in wood and time has swallowed up the palaces and temples, leaving only the story-telling of the *wayang golek* (wooden-puppet show), enduring folk beliefs, and the secrets of the reclusive Badui people as testimony to a time before Islam.

West Coast

The coastline from Anyer to Labuhan is less than three hours from Jakarta. **Carita Beach** is the oldest seaside resort on the west coast. There are several hotels here, overlooking a crescent-shaped bay with silver sand and safe swimming. From here, the ruins of the medieval trading city of Banten can be explored in a day-trip: it has a 16th-century mosque and fascinating remains of palaces and forts.

Krakatau (Krakatoa) ★★★

The original island of Krakatau was vaporized in 1883 in a series of catastrophic explosions heard as far away as Alice Springs in Australia. But this was not its end. In 1928 the mountain was reborn, emerging from the seas as **Anak Krakatau** ('Child of Krakatau'). It continues to grow, and is now more than 200m (700ft) high. It still has spectacular eruptions. It is sometimes possible to climb the mountain in a long, hot and dusty slog – but be aware that tourists have been killed in unexpected eruptions. It is a long, hot and dusty climb to a ridge close to the crater. The volcano is surrounded by three smaller islands, surviving fragments of the 1883 cataclysm.

Ujung Kulon National Park ★★

The Ujung Kulon peninsula was deserted by humans after the 1883 tsunami resulting from the eruption of Krakatau. It is the only place where a viable population of Javan rhinos exists – there are around 60 of them. Other animals include leopards, Javan gibbons, wild cattle (banteng), muntjac and sambar deer and green peafowl. Turtles nest in some of the sandy bays.

Bogor

Sprawling over a plateau and now almost merged with Jakarta, Bogor was a tiny hill village until selected by the Dutch in 1745 as the seat of the first Governor-General of Java. His magnificent palace, the glowing white **Istana Bogor**, now houses Sukarno's collection of erotic art. Known to the Dutch as Buitenzorg ('away from cares'), the city has grown up around the magnificent botanical gardens or **Kebun Raya**. Most tours also take in the **Batu Tulis**, an ancient stone with Sanskrit inscriptions. Beware of the daily thunderstorms complete with torrential rain – not for nothing is Bogor known as 'City of Rain'!

Natural History Museum ★

Particularly impressive is the entire skeleton of a Blue whale and a display of Indonesia's venomous snakes. More depressing are the stuffed remains of a Javan tiger (extinct), and a Javan rhino. The (fake) horns on stuffed rhino specimens are repeatedly stolen – an indication of the poaching threat confronting Indonesia's rhinos.

From Bogor

Head south to the **Puncak** (*puncak* means 'peak') district to enjoy glorious mountain landscapes and cool air. The scenery is lush and rich, dominated by volcanoes like **Mt Gede** and **Mt Pangrango**, their slopes planted with tea gardens and dotted with bubbling hot springs and good hotels. The **Cibodas Botanical Gardens** are the high-altitude section of Bogor's Kebun Raya and are adjacent to the **Gunung Gede–Pangrango National Park**. Trails here lead amongst well-tended flowers-beds, or up mountain slopes in the national park. Even a day trip here gives a good idea of the rainforest, and for the visitor with more time to spare there are wonderful views and rare plants including giant edelweiss 8m (26ft) high.

Below: *Anak Krakatau, the new island rebuilding itself on the site of the volcano that erupted so spectacularly – and so tragically – in 1883.*

Above: *A traditional Javanese* gamelan *player.*

HILL FRUIT

The hills around Bandung are high enough to grow European fruits and vegetables, including strawberries (delicious) and apples (rather woolly).

From Puncak, take a narrow winding road through the hills to the fishing village of **Pelabuhanratu**, where there are lovely beaches between rocky headlands, holy caves with bats streaming forth like smoke at sunset, and excellent fish restaurants. Be careful swimming here: this is the domain of Nyai Loro Kidul, Queen of the South Seas.

Bandung

Java's third-largest city, Bandung is home to the **Institute of Technology**, one of Indonesia's best universities, and dozens of other research and teaching institutes. Bandung hosts a cocktail of cultural events – from Indonesian jazz and rock concerts to classical *wayang golek* puppet performances and traditional Sundanese dance and music. It is a pleasant city with many colonial buildings, but like all big Indonesian cities staggers under the weight of traffic.

The most interesting museums are the **Sundanese Museum of Art** and the neighbouring **Museum of West Java**, in Jl Otista. The **Geological Museum** in Jl Diponegoro is worth a look – displays include a fossil skull of Java Man (*Homo erectus*) and good pictures of volcanic eruptions. Have dinner in the wonderful Art Nouveau dining-room of the Savoy Homann Hotel, one of the great hotels of Asia.

West Java is the home of *wayang golek*, or wooden puppets. Performances are usually held Friday and Saturday in the **Gedung Kesenian** – those who lack the stamina for an all-night show can drop out after an hour or two. **Rumentang Siang Theatre** (Jl Ahmad Yani) stages *wayang*, dance and drama almost every night. The **Yayasan Pusat Kebudayaan** (Jl Naripan 7; off busy Jl Braga) puts on *gamelan* or *wayang* most evenings. **Sindeng Reret Restaurant** (Jl Naripan 9) has shorter *wayang golek* shows most Saturdays. **Hotel Panghegar** and **Hotel Grand Preanger** stage cultural performances at least once a week with a variety of dance, music and *wayang* – one-stop culture with dinner.

Visit **Pak Ujo's 'Bamboo Workshop'** to hear the sweet, hollow sounds of the *anklung*, or bamboo orchestra. Students at **ASTI**, the Academy of Performing Arts (Jl Buah Batu 212), often stage dance performances and concerts, and welcome interested visitors any time.

TAXI OR TOUR?

Chartering a taxi for three or four people is often cheaper than booking a tour, and allows you to be more flexible. English-speaking drivers are often quite knowledgeable.

Around Bandung

Head into the hills for stunning mountain scenery, active volcanoes, bubbling hot springs and mud pools. **Tangkubahan
Prahu**, about an hour north of Bandung, is Indonesia's only
drive-in volcano; visit early before the crowds and the clouds
arrive, and take a guide if you want to explore the craters –
the crust on some is thin. On your way back, make a detour
to **Ciater** via a huge tea estate and visit the nearby hot
springs at **Maribaya**. From Maribaya there is an easy 3-hour
walk back to Bandung through beautiful countryside: the
path is straightforward and well-maintained (a small charge
is levied by villagers who look after th trail). The walk ends
at Dago, a suburb of Bandung, and you can finish off with
some refreshments at the quaint Dago Tea-house.

    Papandayan volcano, near Cisurupan, south of
Bandung, has spectacular geysers and is less commercial
than Tangkubahan Prahu. The surrounding area is beautiful and tranquil. On your way back from Papandayan, visit
the **Malabar Tea Estate**, near Pangalengan.

From Bandung

The road east from Bandung to Garut travels past volcanoes, beautiful lakes and relics of Java's Hindu and
Buddhist past. The small temple complex at **Situ Cangkuang**
(20min from Garut) dates back to at least the 9th century AD.
Continuing east to Yogyakarta, the road takes you through
the junction town of **Tasikmalaya**, famous for its hats,
woven rattan baskets and pretty hand-painted umbrellas. At
Banjarnegara (Banjar), allow yourself to be tempted by the
beach and head south (2 hours) to **Pangandaran**.

Pangandaran ★★

Two beautiful beaches, a nature reserve, friendly
fishermen and delicious seafood … it is easy to
stay longer in Pangandaran than you planned. The
village is at the neck of a narrow peninsula, now a
national park. Fishermen mend their nets on the
beaches to the east, while tourists drowse in the
sun on the beaches to the west. At peak holiday
times the area becomes busy with local tourists.

CROWDED ROADS

At weekends the roads to
and from the West Java
resorts are packed with
trippers from Jakarta, so
allow plenty of time.

GOING BY TRAIN

Although a fast highway now
links Jakarta and Bandung in
less than two hours, the
nicest way to travel here is
by train (3 hours; several
trains daily) from Jakarta's
Gambir Station. The trains
are slow, rattling and often
late, but from air-conditioned
Executive Class carriages
with their spacious seats
you can enjoy views of
mountains, ravines, waterfalls and tiny villages. Train
schedules can be found on
www.kereta-api.com

Below: *Fishing boats on
Java's west coast seem to
have changed little with
the centuries.*

HIGH ALTITUDE

At over 2000m (6500ft) above sea level, Dieng and Bromo can get extremely chilly, particularly Jun–Sep, with sometimes even a night frost.

BREAK THE JOURNEY

Stay overnight in pleasant Wonosobo in the valley below Dieng Plateau rather than making the 6-hour round trip from Yogyakarta in a day. The marathon day trips offered by tour operators in Yogyakarta, taking in both Dieng and Borobudur, are strictly for those very pressed for time.

Below: *A wry smile from one of the retainers at the Kraton in Yogyakarta.*

Pangandaran National Park

There is good snorkelling off the peninsula's beaches and turtles can occasionally be spotted in the pretty coves near **Pasir Putih**. In the park are black leaf-monkeys, semi-tame deer, hornbills sounding like a steam train in flight, and banteng feeding in open clearings in the late afternoon. You have to get a permit and take a guide – try and find an older one who knows the animals' feeding and movement patterns.

A popular excursion from Pangandaran is the Green Canyon tour, covering small, homely factories making palm-sugar and *krupuk* (prawn crackers), a wayang golek workshop, and a boat-ride upriver into steep-sided gorges which become a giant cavern. Swimming through the clear turquoise water and leaping from rocks into a deep plunge-pool are unforgettable experiences.

From Pangandaran

Instead of doubling back to Banjar to rejoin the road or take a train to Yogyakarta, go to **Kalipucing** and catch the ferry to **Cilacap**. The journey is four hours of magic through coastal waterways and mangrove swamps – wonderful for bird-watchers, who should see herons, sea-eagles, cormorants, kingfishers and more. Pangandaran hotels organize ferry tickets and operate a private Cilacap–Yogyakarta minibus service (5 hours) linked to the ferry's arrival. An alternative is to travel from Cilacap to **Wonosobo** (2 hours), the access point for Dieng Plateau.

Dieng Plateau ★★

Less visited than Java's other great temple sites, Dieng has been a holy place for centuries. The name means 'Abode of the Gods', and in the early morning, with the ground mist swirling about you, there is a haunting, otherworldly atmosphere. Of a city with more than 400 Shiva temples and massive flights of steps rising from the valley below, today only eight small temples survive, marooned in a strange, wild landscape of bubbling mud pools, crater lakes and hot springs.

Central Java

This is the Java of the imagination, a land of volcanoes towering over fertile plains dotted with thousand-year-old temples and half-forgotten shrines, a land where *gamelan* orchestras play in royal courts whose rulers trace their line back to a sea goddess – and where some of the finest crafts of the archipelago are produced.

Yogyakarta

For centuries Yogyakarta (Yogya – now often written Jogja) was a royal kingdom and powerful trading centre, the seat of the powerful Mataram Empire. The patina of power and pride built up over the centuries still lingers. Today Yogya is best known as a city of culture and the arts. Explore the narrow side streets to see craftsmen producing exquisite batik and silverwork, visit the Batik Research Centre to see how the craft is being fostered, or haunt the **Kraton** (palace) to watch some of Indonesia's finest dancers and musicians.

The attractions are not only within the city's boundaries. **Borobudur** is less than 2 hours away, while the fantastic temples of **Prambanan** are within half an hour. The energetic can climb one of Indonesia's most iconic (but dangerous) volcanoes, **Mt Merapi** (2911m; 9550ft), menacingly visible from the city. In May 2006 Yogya was struck by an earthquake in which around 5000 people died and many buildings collapsed; empty building plots you see may be due to this.

Palaces ★★★

The **Kraton** (palace) is effectively a city in itself, with batik and silver workshops, mosques, shops and schools enclosed within the remains of 3m (10ft) thick walls. Highlights include the throne-room, ancient *gamelan* and two museums. Classical dance performances and *gamelan* concerts are staged here at least once a week (not during Ramadan).

Taman Sari (the Water Palace), is a series of pleasure gardens built in the 18th century for the sultan and his family. The complex once boasted lighted underwater corridors, underground mosques and meditation platforms.

Pakualaman Palace is smaller but still a fine *kraton*. *Gamelan* concerts are held here usually once a month.

Below: *The magnificent headdress of a dancer in Yogyakarta.*

Loro Kidul and the Sultans of Yogya

According to legend, the Sultans of Yogya descend from a mystical union between the mortal Senopati and the Queen of the Southern Seas, Nyai Loro Kidul. The reigning sultan still pays tribute to Loro Kidul each year with offerings to the goddess at Parangritis in June (the Labuhan festival) and ceremonies on the slopes of Mt Merapi, and she is said to appear sometimes during the sacred Bedoyo Ketawang dance, performed in her honour in the Kraton.

Sonobudoyo Museum, on the square to the north of the Kraton (the Alun-alun), has a comprehensive collection of Javanese arts and crafts. Visit here before you buy batik or other crafts so you can gauge quality.

Cultural Performances

There is a bewildering array of locations for the performing arts of Yogya – from palace to university auditorium to street corner, or your hotel lobby. See classical Javanese ballet, marvellous, intricate *gamelan* concerts, wonderful *wayang kulit* plays and even *wayang orang*, in which people play the parts usually taken by puppets.

Seize any chance to see an episode of the **Ramayana Ballet**. The most magnificent location is the outdoor arena at Prambanan with the floodlit Shiva temple as backdrop. Dozens of fantastically costumed actors and musicians enact the epic, staged around the full moon in each month May–October. The full event runs over the course of four evenings; shorter versions are staged all over Yogyakarta.

Around Yogya

Kota Gede was the capital of the Mataram Empire in the 16th century but is now a suburb of Yogya and a centre of fine silverwork. Near the market is the **grave of Senopati**, who founded the city. **Imogiri** (20min) is the burial-place of the royal family and of many sultans of Solo. **Parangtritis** (30min) is a popular beach and centre for the cult of Loro Kidul; offerings are made to the goddess each week. The sea is dangerous – she has set up a strong undertow.

Prambanan

Ranked with Borobudur by many art historians, the Buddhist and Hindu temple complexes of the Prambanan Plain are among the finest flowerings of ancient Javanese architecture. Yet soon after completion, in the 8th–10th centuries, they were abandoned and all but forgotten. Today the major temples have been restored although scores remain to be excavated.

Temple Complex ★★★

Candi Lorojonggrang is the largest and most spectacular of the Hindu temples on the Prambanan Plain. The **Shiva Temple**, 45m (150ft) tall, is the showpiece: it was damaged during the 2006 earthquake, but is being rebuilt. It is flanked by the smaller but still magnificent Brahma, Vishnu and Nandi temples. The interior chambers are wonderfully carved and decorated with tales from the *Ramayana*.

Walk or take an open-sided bus from Candi Lorojonggrang to **Candi Sewu**, Indonesia's second-largest Buddhist temple complex after Borobudur and now restored to part of its former glory. 'Candi Sewu' means '1000 temples'; in fact the complex consists of 249 shrines surrounding the major temple, which dates back to AD782 and is protected by huge guardian statues.

Other Prambanan Sites ★★

Hire a car (or a bicycle) for the day to explore the dozens of other temple sites around Prambanan. They include:

Candi Lumbung, a 10-minute walk from Candi Lorojonggrang. A small Buddhist temple surrounded by partly restored shrines.

Candi Sari, on the road from Yogya to Prambanan. Famous for its decorated and carved panels.

Candi Kalasan, just off the main Yogya–Solo road before Prambanan. The oldest temple of known date (AD778) Buddhist temple in Indonesia.

Below: *Visitors approaching the imposing entrance to Yogyakarta's Kraton.*

Opposite: *Startlingly
evocative, the figure of
the Buddha silhouetted
against the darkling sky at
Borobudur.*

Lush gardens surround these temples. Other sites worth
a look include **King Boku's temple** at Ratu Boku, where
excavation and restoration continue, and nearby **Candi
Banyunibo**.

Borobudur ★★★

The world's largest Buddhist temple and the greatest ancient
monument in the southern hemisphere, Borobudur is one of
the wonders of the world, an artificial mountain of some
60,000m³ (2 million cu ft) of stone. It was built between 778
and 850 – and abandoned soon after completion when the
Buddhist Sailendra dynasty was overthrown by Hindu kings.
Borobudur was all but forgotten, buried – and protected – by
ash from successive eruptions of Mt Merapi until its rediscov-
ery in the early 19th century. Over the next century restoration work was undertaken, and in the mid-1960s a huge
archaeological rescue project was launched by UNESCO. In
a task comparable with the resiting of Egypt's Abu Simbel statues, Borobudur was quite literally taken to pieces and rebuilt.

The temple was constructed to resemble India's sacred
Mount Meru, with a series of square and circular terraces
linked by four main stairways. By turning left upon entering
and circumnavigating each tier, you follow the pilgrims'
path to the summit, a symbolic journey through the three
spheres of Tantric Buddhism. The 5km (3-mile) walk takes
you past 1500 relief carvings of the Buddha's teachings and
1200 purely decorative panels. The carvings, a textbook of
life in 8th- and 9th-century Java, are studied by historians
as well as art lovers.

On the upper, open terraces are more than 70
stupas, most containing sitting statues of the young
Buddha. Many of the heads are missing, taken over the
centuries by collectors or smashed by fundamentalist
Muslims during the 1980s.

En route for Borobudur, stop at **Mendut**. The temple here
has a statue of the seated Buddha flanked by two acolytes.

Solo (Surakarta)

Vying with Yogya as Java's cultural capital, Solo has all the
attractions of its rival: *wayang* theatres and *gamelan*

orchestras, wonderful crafts and good food, and two *kratons* – one even larger and older than Yogya's.

Kraton Hadiningrat was badly damaged by fire in the mid-1980s but has been restored. In the palace museum look for Hindu figurines, wedding carriages and a huge wooden statue once carried on the royal barge. The meditation tower was used by the Sultan when he communed with Nyai Loro Kidul. **Kraton Mangkunegaran**, a 10-minute stroll from the main palace, belongs to a junior line of the Solo royal family. Dating from 1757, it hosts one of Java's oldest *gamelan* orchestras, **Jyai Kanyut Mesem** ('Drifting with Smiles'). For most visitors, the museum is the real delight, with wonderful costumes, an excellent collection of masks and a few strange items – including a silver chastity belt. **Radya Pustaka Museum**, next to Sriwedari Park, was founded in the 1890s as the Institute of Javanese Culture and has an excellent collection of old *kris* (wavy-bladed daggers) and local crafts.

From Solo

Sangiran is the site where the first relics of *Homo erectus* were unearthed. A good museum has some interesting exhibits. Java's only erotic temple, **Sukuh** lies high on the slopes of beautiful **Mt Lawu**, with lovely views over the plains. There are good walks in the area, especially the path to Tawang-mangu, emerging by the huge **Grojogan Sewu** waterfalls. A short drive from Sukuh is another Hindu temple, **Candi Ceto**; beautifully restored, it is built in a series of terraces up a mountainside, with breathtaking views.

East Java

Most visitors race through East Java en route for the beaches of Bali, pausing briefly at **Mount Bromo**. But it is definitely worth lingering a little, especially around the hill city of **Malang**.

MUSIC AND DANCE IN SOLO

Like Yogya, Solo hosts a dazzling array of arts and entertainments. Ask at the Tourist Office at Jl Slamet Riyadi 275 (closed Sundays). Performances of court dances, less formal than in Yogya, are held each week at **Kraton Mangkunegaran** (usually Wednesday mornings). Further fine dance and music can be seen at **ASKI**, the conservatory of music and dance. The **Wayang Orang Sriwedari** troupe perform most nights in **Sriwedari Park**. Alternatively, just relax and listen to the nightly *gamelan* concerts at the **Kusuma Sahid Prince Hotel**, which also stages *wayang orang* on occasion. As in most cities, the local Radio Republik Indonesia station sponsors regular cultural events from *wayang kulit* to classical dance.

Below: *Bull-racing on the island of Madura.*

Surabaya

Surabaya, capital of East Java, is Indonesia's second-largest city. The city administration is doing its best to keep the older parts of the city well-kept: there are wide streets in the Jembatan Merah area with some fine neoclassical, Art Deco, Arts and Crafts and Art Nouveau buildings. **Surabaya Zoo** has a good collection of Indonesian fauna, particularly birds. Look for the beautiful white Bali starlings (*Leucopsar rothschildi*), one of the world's rarest birds, which breeds easily in captivity, but is almost extinct in the wild because of over-trapping for the caged trade. **Perak Harbour** has many traditional craft, including Buginese *pinisi* and schooners from neighbouring Madura.

Exploring East Java from Surabaya has been made considerably harder by the 'Lapindo mudflow', with millions of litres of hot, acrid mud spewing from a fault in the Earth's crust. It started in May 2006 and shows no sign of stopping. The motorway south of Surabaya has been destroyed, and people are starting to use Malang airport as a hub to reach places to the south and east of Surabaya.

Madura

The island of Madura has fine beaches, ancient mosques and friendly people. But its real attraction is the bull-racing (*kerapan sapi*). Events are held at least twice a month between April and October with the championships staged in October in **Pamekasan**. Up to 24 pairs of specially bred racing bulls take part in each event, covering 100m (110yd) in just nine seconds.

Malang

Malang is pleasantly cooler than Surabaya, with magnificent scenery nearby. The town has some lovely colonial buildings and is well situated for exploring East Java's ancient temple sites, dating from the Hindu-Buddhist period.

Malang also offers an alternative entry point to the Bromo Tengger Semeru National Park. It is a two-hour drive to

Ngadas, a tiny traditional hill village, and then a half-day walk to Mt Bromo or to Ranu Pani. Ranu Pani is the base for treks up Mt Semeru, Java's highest peak (3676m, 12,060ft). There is excellent trekking all around the hills and valleys here – but stick to the paths or take a guide. It is easy to lose your way.

Kaliandra

Between Surabaya and Malang, Kaliandra (near Prigen) is a good base for exploring the mountains and cultural sites. There are some fine temples nearby, including beautiful **Candi Jawi** and **Candi Singosari**. Finest perhaps is **Candi Kidal**, a tall, ornately carved 13th-century shrine which has been sensitively restored. Further afield (a full day's trip) is **Candi Penataran**, East Java's biggest temple complex. Near Kaliandra is the Cisarua Safari Park, worth a visit to see animals from Indonesia and elsewhere (including elephants and tigers) roaming in relative freedom. Take the mountain road via Kediri towards Blitar for fantastic scenery and stop in Blitar for a typical, unpretentious small Javanese town.

Mt Bromo ★★★

Rightly one of Indonesia's great draws, Mt Bromo is best at dawn in the dry season, when it becomes a place where dreams catch fire. The volcano lies marooned with its extinct neighbour **Batok** in a sea of ash and lava, the Sand Sea, within the caldera of the huge, ancient Tengger volcano. It is an eerie place, especially at night as you cross the Sand Sea to the 250 steep steps leading to the crater lip. As the sun rises over the lava fields, illuminating massive **Mt Semeru** in the distance, silence falls and the power and beauty of nature strike home. To avoid the crowds but still see spectacular views, visit the crater just after sunrise when everyone else has left.

Bromo is surrounded by the villages of the Tengger people, who farm temperate crops such as potatoes and leeks. The Tenggerese are the only inhabitants of Java to have retained the Hindu faith which dominated the island until the 16th century.

KASADA FESTIVAL

A number of ceremonies are held at Bromo, many involving sacrifices to pacify the volcano. Most famous is the Kasada, when thousands of people climb the volcano to commemorate their ancestors. Fruit, flowers, chicken and even live water-buffalo are thrown into the crater ... or at least into the arms of waiting supplicants – a mutually beneficial arrangement. The date changes each year.

THE FAR EAST

There are several good wildlife reserves in East Java. Most accessible is **Baluran National Park**, easily reached from Ketapang, ferry port for Bali, or on the way to Bali from Bromo. The varied vegetation and open savanna offer good wildlife viewing, although acacia trees are encroaching on the grasslands. Less easily reached is **Meru Betiri National Park**, on the south coast, established in a vain attempt to save the last Javan tigers. The main attraction now is a turtle-nesting beach at **Sukamade**, and the rainforest is still dense and packed with birdlife.

Jakarta at a Glance

GETTING AROUND

Allow plenty of time to get around: Jakarta's traffic is heavy all day. Taxis are inexpensive and metered – Golden Bird and Silver Bird are the best (they wait at hotels and the airport or can be ordered by phone). *Bajaj* (pronounced 'badjay') – two-seater three-wheeled cabs, less comfortable than taxis and terribly noisy – are fine for short distances. Because Jakarta's traffic can be at a near standstill from early morning to late evening, it can be swifter to catch one of the air-conditioned buses that speed along busways past the stationary cars. *From Jakarta's Sukarno-Hatta Airport:* Registered taxis queue outside the arrivals hall. Unless you know how much the fare should be, shun the pirate cab drivers offering a 'cheaper' deal. The Damri airport bus service into the city is inexpensive and reliable; one route goes straight to Gambir Station. Major hotels operate courtesy bus services. Count on an hour into town, but at least 90min to reach the airport from Central Jakarta during the rush hour. If offered a choice by the driver, always choose the expressway (pay for tolls separately from the fare).

Getting Away

By air: Domestic and international flights depart from Sukarno–Hatta.
By train: From Gambir Station to Bogor (90min), Bandung (3hr) and Yogyakarta

(10–12hr). The night expresses to Surabaya (via Yogyakarta) depart from Kota Station. Don't waste time queuing for tickets – book through a travel agent.

WHERE TO STAY

Most tourist and international hotels are centred on Jl Thamrin and its extension Jl Sudirman, the city's main north-south roads. If you are only in transit, stay at the Aspac Quality Hotel, tel: (021) 559 0008, at Terminal Two, or at the airport Sheraton Bandara Hotel.

LUXURY

Borobudur InterContinental, Jl Lapangan Banteng Selatan, tel: (021) 380 5555, fax: (021) 380 9595, www.hotel borobudur.com North of the Central Business District, with everything from Olympic-size pool to jogging track.
Le Meridien, Jl Sudirman 18-20, tel: (021) 251 3131, fax: (021) 571 1633. In the Central Business District.
Hotel Mulia, Jl Asia Afrika Senayan, tel: (021) 574 7777, fax: (021) 574 7888. Plushly opulent in reds and golds.
Sutlan Hotel, Jl Garot Subroto, tel: (021) 570 3600, fax: (021) 573 3089, www.sultanjakarta.com
Hotel Indonesia, Jl Thamrin, tel: (021) 230 1008, fax: (021) 230 1007. The oldest luxury hotel in Jakarta, opp the British Embassy (renovated in 2007).

MID-RANGE

Atlet Century Park, Jl Pintu Satu Senayan, tel: (021) 571 2041, fax: (021) 571 2191.

Centrally located and overlooking a large park.
Grand Kemang Hotel, Jl Kemang Raya 2H, tel: (021) 719 4121, fax: (021) 799 3492. Further south in Jakarta and good for access to Taman Mini and Bogor.
Hotel Menteng I, Jl Gondangdia Lama 28, tel: (021) 310 6468; fax (021) 3144151). Away from busiest business districts, reasonable quality, sensible price.
Ibis Tamarind, Jl Wahid Hasyim 77, tel: (021) 315 7706, fax: (021) 315 7707. North Jakarta.
Hotel Garden, Jl Kemang Raya Kebayoran Baru, tel: (021) 798 0760, fax: (021) 798 0760). South Jakarta.

WHERE TO EAT

Jakarta has no shortage of excellent restaurants serving food from around the world. Do try the street stalls – anything cooked in front of you is pretty safe. The closest night food stalls to Jl Thamrin are on Jl Agus Salim, parallel to and east of Jl Thamrin. Also visit the basement of any of the big malls, where street food is prepared in hygienic surroundings and you can select from several different types of food. For more formal meals, try:
The Oasis, Jl Raden Saleh Raya 47, tel: (021) 315 0646. Famous for its *Rijstafel* and stylish surroundings. Booking is essential.
Dragon City Seafood Restaurant, Lippo Plaza

Jakarta at a Glance

Podium Block, ground floor, Jl Sudirman Kav. 25, tel: (021) 522 1933.
Kemang Chinese and Seafood, Jl Kemang Raya, tel: (021) 719 3854.
Dapur Sunda, Jl Cipete Raya 13, tel: (021) 769 4834.
Pulau Dua, Taman Ria Senayan, Jl Gatot Subroto, tel: (021) 570 8906/7. Popular open-air Indonesian restaurant near the Hilton Hotel and Taman Ria Senayan.
Jakarta Restaurant, Dharma-wangsa Hotel, Jl Brawidjaja Raya 26, Kebayoran Baru, tel: (021) 725 8181.
Sate Khas Senayan, Jl Pakubuwono VI/6, Kebayoran Baru, tel: (021) 725 0324.
Ikan Bakar Kebon Sirih, Jl Kebon Sirih, above the excellent **Shalimar Indian Restaurant**, serves barbecued and baked fish.
Jakarta's international-class hotels serve first-rate food. Try: **Bengawan Solo**, at the Sahid Jaya Hotel, Jl Jend Sudirman 86, tel: (021) 570 4444.
Nippon-Kan, at the Hilton, Japanese food – try also the Hilton's Pizzeria, with live bands, and the Taman Sari, among the city's top French restaurants.
Nelayan, at the Borobudur InterContinental, seafood.

TRADITIONAL ENTERTAINMENT

Bharata Theatre (Jl Kalilio 156, Pasar Senen) offers excellent *wayang orang* (dance) dramas nightly except Monday and Thursday. The **National**
Museum** and **Wayang Museum** stage superb *wayang kulit* (shadow puppet), *wayang golek* (wooden puppet) and *gamelan* performances on Sunday mornings. **Hotel Borobudur** is among the international-class hotels to stage traditional dance and music: book for Saturday night dinner and the show is included. Batak singers from Sumatra are known for their harmonies: groups of them serenade diners at several restaurants in the city.

SHOPPING

With arts and crafts from all over the archipelago and huge shopping malls rivalliing the best in Asia, Jakarta is a shopa-holic's paradise. There is good handicraft shopping at **Sarinah Department Store**, Jl Thamrin. Prices for handicrafts, batik and designer clothes by top Indonesian fashion houses are fixed and reasonable, and the quality is good.

The **Ratu Plaza** mall, in South Jakarta, specializes in computer and electronic goods. **Pasar Seni**, in Ancol, north Jakarta, offers arts/handi-crafts. **Pasar Tanah Abang** specializes in textiles. The **Jakarta Handicraft Centre** (Jl Pekalongan 12, near the Hotel Indonesia) sells crafts from across Indonesia. **Keris Gallery** (Jl Cokroaminoto 87) has good batik, handicrafts and women's clothes. Other malls are Pondok Indah Mall (I and II), Plaza Indonesia (try Baca Ratu in the basement
food hall for good Padang food), Taman Anggrek Ione of the largest malls in Southeast Asia), Senayan City, and Plaza Semanggi. Full of international brands selling goods more cheaply than in Europe, most malls have a mix of shops and entertainment facilities designed to attract the world traveller. Security is good. Best time to shop is soon after they open, at 10 – by late afternoon they are crowded with school children and office-workers.
Antiques
Jl Surabaya is Jakarta's most famous flea and antique market. Doubt claims of age and authenticity, and bargain hard.
Jl Kebon Sirih Timur Dalam has many interesting antique shops: haggle, despite pro-prietors' pained looks! **Jl Pelatehan** in the Blok M area is worth checking out but tends to be expensive. For a real treasure hunt, take a taxi to **Situ Gintung** village on Jl Ciputat Raya (1 hour), where the road is lined with scores of antique shops and restorers.

TOURS

Tours of Jakarta or around the country can be arranged through **Iwata Nusantara Tours and Travel**, tel: (021) 8370 0245, www.iwata-travel.com For more adventurous tours, try the well-established **Adventure Indonesia**, Wisma 31, Jl Raya Kemang 31, tel: (021) 718 2250, fax: (021) 718 0438, www.adventureindonesia.com

Java at a Glance

GETTING AROUND

A bewildering choice of airlines offer flights linking the major cities. More time-consuming but much more interesting are the trains, which go to all major cities, including Bogor. Cars (with drivers) are easily hired everywhere. In **Yogyakarta** take a *becak* – cycle rickshaw – or horse-drawn *andong* to explore the city (check the going rate with your hotel).

WHERE TO STAY

Carita
Carita Krakatau Hotel, tel: (0253) 83027. Clean and good value.
Krakatau Seaside, tel: (0253) 81081. Lovely individual cottages in the style of traditional Indonesian houses, on the beach. There are many other guesthouses here.

Ujung Kulon National Park
Tourist-class air-conditioned bungalows on Peucang. Tours can be arranged through Black Rhino tour company, tel: (0253) 81072.

Bogor
Hotel Pangrango II, Jl Raya Pajajaran 32, tel: (0251) 312 375, fax: (0251) 377 750.
Abu Pensione Hotel, Jl Mayor Oking, tel: 90251) 322 893. Looks unpromising, but friendly service and adequate rooms, well-priced.

Pelabuhanratu
Samudra Beach Hotel, Jl Raya, tel: (0268) 41200 and 41201,

fax: (0268) 41014. Well away from the village.
Pondok Dewata Cottages, Jl Sirnagalik, tel: (0268) 41531. Nice bungalows with small swimming pool.

Bandung
Grand Hotel Preanger, Jl Asia Afrika 81, tel: (022) 4233 631, fax: (022) 430 034, www.aerowisata.com Beautifully restored colonial-style hotel.
Savoy Homann Hotel, Jl Asia Afrika 112, tel: (022) 432 244, fax: (022) 436 187. Bandung's stateliest and oldest hotel.
Panghegar Heritage Hotel, Jl Merdeka 2, tel: (022) 432 286, fax: (022) 431 583. Outside Bandung, try the Sari Ater Hot Springs Resort at Ciater, tel: (0264) 470 894, with a series of hot springs and waterfalls leading down into the valley.

Pangandaran
Over 40 guesthouses/small hotels. **Hotel Komodo**, Jl Baru Bulak Laut 105, tel: (0265) 630 753, is friendly and clean. **The Sandaan Hotel**, Jl Pamugaran Bulak Lauk, tel: (0265) 639 165 or 639 187, has a swimming pool.

Wonosobo
Hotel Kresna Wonosobo, Jl Pasukan Ronggolawe 30, tel: (0286) 324 111, fax: (0286) 324 112.
Surya Asri Hotel, Jl A Yani 137, tel: (0286) 322 992, fax: (0286) 323 598.

Yogyakarta
Hundreds of hotels and guesthouses here to suit all tastes and pockets.
LUXURY
Ambarrukmo Palace Hotel, Jl Adisucipto Km 5, tel: (0274) 566 488, fax: (0274) 563 283. Out of town towards airport.
Inna Garuda, Jl Malioboro 60, tel: (0274) 566 353, fax: (0274) 563 074. A much renovated colonial hotel, very central.
MID-RANGE
Puri Artha, Jl Cendrawasih 36, tel: (0274) 563 288.
BUDGET
Hotel Monica, Jl Sosrowijayan, tel: (0274) 580 598 or try one of the guesthouses around and along Jl Prawirotaman – some are very good value. Most can organize tours, bus and plane tickets.

Solo
Kusuma Sahid Prince, Jl Sugyopranoto 20, tel: (0271) 746 356. Super location, vast pool, nightly *gamelan*.
Kusuma Kartikasari, Jl Sutami 63, tel: (0271) 756 861.
Lor In, Jl Adisucipto 47, tel: (0271) 724 500, fax: (0271) 724 400.
Hotel Quality Solo, Jl Ahmad Yani 40, tel: (0271) 731 312, fax: (0271) 738 677. Good business facilities.

Surabaya
Hyatt Regency Surabaya, Jl Basuki Rachmad 106–128, tel: (031) 531 1234, fax: (031) 532 1508. One of the best hotels in Indonesia.

Java at a Glance

Majapahit Mandarin Oriental, Jl Tunjungan 65, tel: (031) 545 4333. Fine old colonial hotel. **Novotel Surabaya,** Jl Ngagel 173–175, tel: (031) 568 2301. **Surabaya Youth Hostel,** Jl Darmo Kali 35, tel: (031) 567 0954. Budget. Air-conditioned, quiet and fairly clean.

An excellent restaurant in Surabaya for Indonesian food is **Dapur Desa,** Jl Basuki Rachmat 72, tel: (031) 546 3999.

Malang
Pelangi Hotel, Jl Merdeka Seletan 3, tel: (0341) 365 156. **Hotel Tugu Malang,** Jl Tugu 3, tel: (0341) 363 891, fax: (0341) 362 747. Upmarket. **Hastinapura,** Kaliandra Foundation, tel: (0343) 417 358, fax: (0343) 417 357, or e-mail: kalian@indo.net.id Lovely guesthouses near Prigen in the hills.

Mt Bromo
Best are the **Lava View Lodge,** tel: (0335) 541 009, and the **Bromo Permai,** tel: (0335) 541 021. At Tosari, further away but quieter, stay at the **Bromo Cottages,** Jl Raya Tosari, Pasuruan, tel: (031) 515 259.

SHOPPING

Bogor
Hand-carved *wayang golek* puppets, gongs, bamboo flutes.

Yogyakarta
Fantastic *batik*, hand-tooled leather, *wayang kulit* puppets, silver, antiques (some genuine), clothes, paintings.

Yogyakarta Craft Centre (by the Ambarrukmo Palace) has fixed prices; look here first to check prices before going to the markets. The Jogja Craft Natural House, at Jl Desa Wisata Kasongan, Tirtonirmolo, Kasihan (tel: 0274 748 0869) has a great variety of souvenirs and larger items such as teak furniture. For silver go to **Kota Gede,** for instance the factory at Jl Mondorakan 1, tel: (0274) 375 107). **Moyudan** village has fine wood carvings. **Jalan Malioboro** has some good items hidden among the tat. Explore the fantastic **Pasar Beringhardjo** (behind Jl Malioboro), a mass of stalls. Many young batik artists work around the **Taman Sari** area. You will be approached by touts trying to entice you to the workshop of their brother/cousin/uncle – this can be a nice way to buy things since you can then picture where they were made. But beware of fake *batiks* (i.e. printed, not drawn). A good (and honest) art shop is the Satria Gallery at Jl Rotowijayan KP II/64, tel: (081) 128 6743. They sell an excellent range of *batiks*, masks, *wayang kulit*, and other Javanese artefacts.

Bandung
Wayang puppets and masks, superb ceramics (convincing copies of ancient Chinese porcelain), paintings, sculpture; musical instruments.

Solo
Jl Secoyudan has goldsmiths' shops. Visit **Sriwedari Park** for presents (especially handmade toys), antiques – from genuine to obviously fake – and handicrafts in the **Pasar Triwindu** fleamarket. There are handmade *wayang kulit* puppets at **Manyaran**, where a dozen or so craftsmen work. For batik visit **Pasar Klewer**, near Susuhunan Palace.

Surabaya
Surabaya has huge shopping centres such as **Tunjungan Plaza** and **Delta Plaza. Jl Basuki Rachmat** is good for curios and antiques. Also worth a visit is the colourful **Kayoon Flower Market.**
For **Krakatau,** hotels in Carita can organize tours. At **Bogor** the tourist office, Jl Veteran 2, just off Jl Juanda, has a great range of excursions and activities; useful maps. In **Bandung** the tourist offices are Bandung Visitor Centre, Jl Asia Afrika, tel: (022) 446 644, and West Java Tourist Office, Jl Cipaganti 15. The **Wonosobo** tourist office, Gedung Sasana Bhakti 45, has maps, suggested walks, and lists of nearby attractions. In **Yogyakarta** the tourist office is at Jl Malioboro 16, tel: (0274) 566 000. The **Solo** tourist office is at Jl Slamet Riyadi 275. The **Surabaya** tourist office, Jl Pemuda 118, tel: (031) 567 5448, has information on events such as Madura bullraces. The **Malang** tourist office is at Jl Tugu 1.

5
Bali

The shimmering green jewel in Indonesia's crown of islands, Bali has epitomized tropical paradise for decades. This is an island of soaring volcanoes, of rice terraces tumbling down the hillsides in sculpted tiers, of fantastic Hindu temples and age-old dances, of glorious beaches and sybaritically luxurious hotels, most nowadays with spas offering all kinds of experiences, from deep-muscle massages to hot stone treatments and clay scrubs.

In the 1930s Bali began to come to the attention of the rest of the world as a series of European artists – like Rudolf Bonnet and Walter Spies – settled here and wrote home with tantalizing pictures of an island paradise in which every man was a painter, sculptor or musician and every woman a dancer.

Religion permeates all aspects of Balinese society: every home and office has a shrine where daily offerings to the spirits are made, and behind every hotel reception desk, on the dash-board of every minibus, one thing remains a constant – a small offering adorned with fresh flowers and rice. The Balinese worship the same trinity – Brahma, Shiva and Vishnu – as Hindus in India, although with the addition of local beliefs. For the Balinese, gods and good spirits live in the mountains while demons and giants lurk in the sea; they seek to maintain a balance between these two extremes, honouring the good and placating the evil. There are temples everywhere. Most villages have at least three: a *pura puseh*, dedicated to the founders of the village, a *pura desa*, for the spirits that protect the village, and a *pura dalem*, the temple of the dead.

CLIMATE

The rainy season runs roughly Nov–Mar, with the heaviest rainfall in Dec–Jan. May–Sep is generally dry, with brilliant blue skies – although expect a few tropical downpours, usually in the late afternoon. But there is another factor to consider when timing your visit: of the island's annual two-million-plus visitors, most descend in Jul, Aug and Dec.

Opposite: *The main street of a Balinese village shows in microcosm that this is an island like no other!*

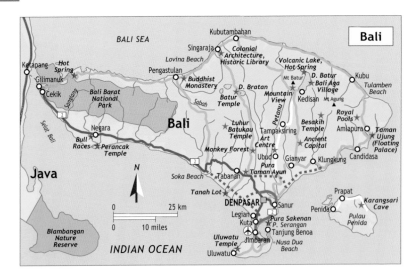

DON'T MISS

** Lake Bratan: A glorious crater lake with, nearby, a temple dedicated to the goddess of the waters.
*** Besakih Temple: Imposingly austere, set amid a fabulous landscape.
*** Lovina Beach: Beautiful beaches with magnificent coral reefs so close you can swim to them.
Tenganan: A fine traditional Bali Aga village where the people are friendly to visitors.

Opposite: *Beauty, youth and grace are just some of the characteristics of Balinese dance.*

Ceremonies and festivals are another integral part of Balinese life and culture, with at least five or six festivals annually in every village. Each stage in life – pregnancy, birth, puberty, marriage and death – has its ritual. Among the best known is the tooth-filing ritual, carried out at puberty, when teeth are filed smooth to produce an even dentition – only demons have crooked fangs. Funerals are spectacular affairs in which the body is carried to its crematory pyre in a bamboo or wooden tower. These may be huge, requiring dozens of men to carry them. The bearers run to the cremation-place, twisting and turning every few metres, moving around in circles – a trick intended to confuse the dead person's spirit so it cannot return to haunt the family.

Balinese Dance

Less formal and more dramatic than the stately court dances of Java, Balinese dance is an art form for the people. Virtually every village has its own dance troupe, and young girls dream of becoming a great Legong dancer. Look out for village festivals, which usually culminate in dance performances. The main dance-forms are:

Kecak: Often called the Monkey Dance, this relates the

legend of the abduction and rescue of Rama's wife Sita. A massed choir – whose monkey-like chanting gives the dance its name – forms the backdrop.

Barong: A brilliant dance narrative that veers from pantomime to high drama as a huge lion-like holy animal (the Barong) does battle with the evil witch Rangda. Best seen in the villages, where people really enter into the spirit.

Legong: Considered by the Balinese the most complex and graceful of all dances. The dancers are usually two young girls who are trained from the age of 5 and retire at 13.

Sanghyang (trance) dances: These probably date back to pre-Hindu exorcism rites. Most spectacular are the Fire Dance, when men trample unharmed on burning coconut shells, and a Legong-style dance in which two young untrained girls dance in unison – with their eyes shut.

THE SOUTH

Bali's main tourist area is centred south of Denpasar, although there are now resorts all over the island. Most of the major temples and craft villages are an easy half-day's excursion from the main resorts.

Denpasar and Surrounds

The island's capital is a working city: noisy and chaotic, but there are several places very much worth visiting. The beautiful **Bali Museum (Museum Negeri)** at Jl Letkol Wisnu 8 (next to Pura Jagatnatha) is built in a series of open pavilions, with examples of both palace (*puri*) and temple (*pura*) architecture. (Open daily; wear long trousers, a sarong or skirt.) The **Art Museum** (Jl Abian Kapas) has three galleries with exhibitions of paintings and woodcarving. Regular dance performances are staged here. In the evenings the **Night Market** behind the Kumbusari Centre has hundreds of stalls selling delicious food.

Not far from Denpasar, **Tanah Lot**, Bali's most photographed sea temple, is a short drive west of Legian. **Pura Taman Ayun**, surrounded by a moat, is the old state temple of the former kingdom of Mengwi and another easy drive from the peninsula. In Sangeh, the temple is just outside the village,

TEMPLES AND PALACES

Bali has an estimated 20,000 temples and palaces. The temples are holy places, so dress appropriately: your legs must be covered. Expect to make a donation when you enter. Menstruating women are not allowed in the temples. Major temples include:

• **Besakih:** The Mother Temple of Bali, on the slopes of sacred Mt Agung. Austere, magnificent.

• **Tanah Lot:** Bali's most famous sea temple, spectacularly sited on an outcrop of rock. Glorious in silhouette at sunset – but crowded.

• **Pura Uluwatu:** Another great sea temple, this literally hangs over the sea. Fantastic sunsets.

• **Tirta Gangga:** One of two water palaces (the other is the Ujung Palace at Karangasem) built in the 20th century by an Amlapuran Sultan.

• **Ulu Danau:** Seems to rise out of Lake Bratan's waters.

• **Kerta Gosa:** At Klungkung, the halls of justice in the days of the rajas. Spectacularly painted ceilings, water gardens and lotus ponds.

VERBAL CONFUSION

The Balinese words for temple and palace are confusingly similar: a *pura* is a temple and a *puri* is a palace.

COCKFIGHTING

Balinese cockfighting is world-famous. Owners of fighting cocks can usually be spotted grooming their birds and planning strategy at the corner of the village market.

UNWANTED DOGS

Bali's legendary mangy dogs have been brought under control in recent years. Don't panic if threatened by one of them – just mime picking up and throwing a stone at it and the dog will vanish at speed. (This works all over Asia.)

Opposite: *The silver sands of Kuta Beach draw holidaymakers from all over the world.*

around 30 minutes from Denpasar. The forest, complete with nutmeg grove, is said to have been dropped by the Monkey God Hanuman as he flew off to do battle with the evil Rawana. Keep a firm hold of your possessions – the monkeys are light-fingered and particularly like spectacles and will snatch them from your face.

Kuta, Legian, Seminyak, Tuban and Jimbaran

Once simple fishing villages set on a palm-fringed beach, **Kuta, Legian** and Seminyak have merged to form Indonesia's biggest resort, with a huge range of hotels. The commercialism can be offputting – although the shopping is excellent. The southern fringes of Kuta are called **Tuban**. To the south of Tuban, on the other side of the airport, **Jimbaran** is a beautiful bay with white-gold sands and several upmarket hotels and spas. Bomb attacks of 2002 and 2005 damaged Indonesia's tourism industry, but the Bali-loving tourists have showed their support by continuing to visit and consistently voting it the best island in the world.

Sanur

Stretching out along a reef-protected beach on the eastern side of the Badung Peninsula, Sanur has attracted Western visitors since the 1930s, when it was a haunt of the artists who 'discovered' Bali. Developed since the 1960s as the smart alternative to Kuta, it now has dozens of luxury hotels running along the coast – although more reasonably priced accommodation can be found here in smaller establishments.

The resort has, though, retained at least some of its Balinese identity. Outrigger canoes are still pulled up on the beach and kite-flying competitions are held in the beach-side fields beyond the hotel strip. There is good 'beginners' snorkelling on the coral reef, but swimming in the shallow bay becomes difficult at low tide. Be careful paddling: coral grazes don't heal easily, and there are sea urchins; also, the coral is easily damaged and can take years to recover from trampling.

The former home of the Belgian artist **Jean Le Mayeur**, who lived in Bali from 1932 till his death in 1958, is now a museum: it is easy to find, right next to the Bali Beach Hotel, built in the early 1960s as the island's first luxury hotel, and the only one taller than a coconut palm.

Nusa Dua

A few miles south of Sanur is Nusa Dua, an enclave of luxury hotels developed to attract the high-spending package tour market. The beaches are good and the hotels are sumptuous, with good shops and restaurants. Tours can be arranged from here to destinations all over Bali and beyond.

Around the Peninsula

Ulu Watu Temple overhangs the towering cliffs at the southern tip of the peninsula. Most people come at sunset, but the temple is spectacular any time. Nearby **Suluban Beach** is said to have the best surf in Bali and regularly features in surfing movies.

Nusa Penida Island, drier and less fertile than the Bali mainland, is visited by thousands of Balinese on pilgrimages to avert bad luck: the island is home to evil spirits. There are a couple of interesting temples and some good beaches, and a turtle conservation programme that hatches and releases baby sea-turtles.

Lembongan, just two hours from Sanur by boat, has become popular with surfers and backpackers. There are some lovely pale gold beaches, good coral and fantastic views of **Mount Agung**.

Ubud

Still with some of the most beautiful scenery in the island peeping between hotels and shops, Ubud is for visitors who want to experience Bali, not just stay in another tropical beach resort. European artists like Spies who settled here in the 1930s encouraged young local artists to break away from the formal Balinese temple and court art and experiment with new images and forms. The village has expanded dramatically: there are now roads and unbroken lines of shops and hotels

MAIN RESORTS

• **Sanur:** Bali's first up-market beach resort, and still quietly stylish. The sea is too shallow to swim at low tide.
• **Nusa Dua:** On the east coast of the southern peninsula, a purpose-built enclave of international-class hotels.
• **The Kuta/Legian strip:** On the southern peninsula's west coast, the liveliest resort. Famous sunsets, surf, shopping and nightlife, but noisy and commercial, and with dangerous waters.
• **Tuban:** To the south of Kuta and slightly quieter and more up-market.
• **Jimbaran:** further south again, with some beautiful beach hotels.
• **Candidasa:** Once a backpackers' haven, now a fully-fledged alternative to Legian and Tuban.
• **Ubud:** Still the cultural heart of the island, set in the hills amid breathtaking scenery, although now a busy town rather than a quiet village and with some nightlife.
• **Lovina:** On the north coast; a slightly more relaxed alternative to the busy southern resorts.

UBUD MARKET

The central market in Ubud functions as a local market for fruit and vegetables from 04:00–06:00, then turns to selling tourist-orientated handicrafts for the rest of the day'.

Below: *In Ubud there are so many dance troupes that it is not hard to find a performance of one of the classics – or even an impromptu street display.*

where 20 years ago there were only rice paddies, and Ubud has merged with surrounding hamlets like **Peliatan**, **Campuhan** and the painting village of **Penestanan**.

Culture still features strongly, however: there are as many art galleries and working studios in Ubud as bars and souvenir shops, and with dozens of local dance troupes, it is easy to find high-class performances of the Balinese classics. In Ubud itself there are performances several nights a week, and tour operators sell transport-inclusive tickets to performances at nearby villages like **Bona** and **Peliatan**. Signboards advertise what is on offer and ticket-sellers tour the streets.

Around Ubud ★★

Puri Lukisan art museum has comprehensive exhibits of all the schools of Balinese painting in a series of pavilions set in lovely gardens. The **Neka Art Museum**, in Campuhan, specializes in modern Balinese art (some pieces are for sale). The well-managed **Monkey Forest**, with its network of paths and polite monkeys which take bananas gently from your fingers, is a 15-minute stroll from the main square, along Monkey Forest Road. There is a small Temple of the Dead in the forest. Follow the paths and steps downhill to find a quiet stream gorge with shrines to the spirits of the springs. **Peliatan**, 2km (just over 1 mile) south of Ubud, is among the most important dance centres in Bali, with two or more performances a week. **Pengosekan** (a 10-minute walk from Peliatan) has many painters; most are delighted to show their work.

One of the nicest expeditions around Ubud is the walk or cycle ride to **Petulu**, where thousands of white egrets roost at night (the birds start to fly in around 16:00). A shorter but no less beautiful walk is down to **Yeh Agung Gorge** at Kedewatan or Sayan. A slightly longer walk on a well-marked trail (take a guide if you are not sure) takes you east from Ubud to the deep **Sungai Petanu** gorge, where you can clamber down to the Goa Gajah cave shrine or walk up to the temples around **Pejeng**.

North of Bali is the **Elephant Safari Park**, with botanical garden and **Sumatran** elephants which give elephant rides.

Bedulu to Tampaksiring ★★★

Between Bedulu and Tampaksiring are more than 30 of Bali's oldest temples and shrines. Explore the area as a day-trip from Ubud: start at Tampaksiring, then slowly make your way back. Many of the paths involve steep climbs up and down.

Gunung Kawi has 11th-century temples and tombs carved into a solid rock face. Get here early to savour the atmosphere. **Tirta Empul** has springs said to prolong life and ease sickness; many Balinese come here on pilgrimage and it can get hectic. In Pejeng, visit **Pura Kebo Edan** ('Crazy Buffalo Temple'), with brilliant carvings and statues, one with six penises. **Pura Penataran Sasih**, the old state temple of Pejeng kingdom, houses the 3m (10ft) long Bronze Age drum known as the **Moon of Pejeng**.

Goa Gajah ('Elephant Cave'), discovered only in the 1920s, was named for the huge demon that forms the temple's mouth. The carvings around the entrance are almost surreal. **Yeh Palu**, a lovely 20min walk (signposted) from Goa Gajah, is more peaceful, a frieze 9m (30ft) long carved on a cliff-face. You might have it to yourself: most tour groups don't walk more than a few metres along the track.

CENTRAL BALI AND THE MOUNTAINS
Mt Batur ★★

You have only to fly over Bali or look at a relief map of the island to realize the central mountains account for much of the territory. The highest – and holiest – point is the currently dormant **Mt Agung** (3142m; 10,308ft). A greater attraction for many is **Mt Batur** (2276m; 7467ft), also a dormant volcano, which towers above Lake Batur and the village of Trunyan.

An easy drive from Ubud or a day-trip from Sanur or Nusa Dua, Mt Batur comprises an ancient caldera out of which a younger volcano (Batur) has risen. **Lake Batur** lies at the foot of the mountain, taking up most of the old caldera. Stop off at **Penelokan**, on the very lip of the old caldera, for fantastic views over the lake. At night (it can be very cold, both here and in Bratan) the moon seems to float on a level with Mt Batur's crater.

Above: *It is not hard to see how Ubud's Lotus Café got its name.*

VILLAGE RETREATS

For a completely relaxing break and escape from the world, stay in villages around Ubud, such as Petulu, Pengosekan and Kedewatan, and learn to make Balinese masks or play the gamelan.

THEMED ARCHITECTURE

Notice the Balinese architectural detail on many modern buildings: cast in concrete, the motifs nevertheless lend a specific stamp to the most mundane of office blocks.

CRAFT VILLAGES

The drive from Denpasar into the hills around Ubud leads through some of Bali's best craft villages. Shops line the main road, but explore the backstreets to see items actually being made.

Batubulan, 10min north of Denpasar, is best known for its stone temple carvings and sculptures, some small enough to consider carrying or shipping home. The village hosts a daily Barong performance which is well choreographed and presented. **Celuk**, beyond Batubulan on the road to Ubud, is Bali's best known silverworking centre; backstreet silversmiths will make pieces to order.

Sukawati is a busy market village, an interesting place to explore, though most coach parties drive straight through on their way to Ubud or Mas. The Pasar Seni art market is worth a look, as are the workshops making wind-chimes and temple umbrellas. The old Sukawati Palace is hidden behind the shops.

Batuan, between Sukawati and Mas, is a painting centre. Shops also sell ornately carved wooden panels and screens. **Mas**, Bali's biggest carving centre, is particularly known for its masks; prices are lower in the afternoon, when the morning coach parties have left. **Gianyar** is the island's biggest weaving centre, with dozens of factories producing everything from traditional sarongs to T–shirts to high fashion items.

Around Lake Batur

Trunyan is a village of the Bali Aga, the original inhabitants of Bali; the lakeside setting is lovely but the villagers do not welcome visitors. The Bali Aga do not cremate their dead but place the body in open bamboo cages to decompose. The graveyard is along the lake (by boat) at **Kuban**.

Tirta, on the lakeshore opposite Trunyan, has hot springs and is a good base for the 3-hour climb to Batur's peak.

Lake Bratan ★★

High in the mountains on one of the few passes through the island, Bratan, like Batur, is a crater lake set in glorious scenery, with tree-covered mountains rising on all sides. It is very peaceful, especially around the nearby smaller lakes (water-skiing is available on the main lake).

Nearby, **Pura Ulu Danau** is dedicated to Dewi Danau, goddess of the waters. The dedication is appropriate: although the main part of the temple is built on a small peninsula, two smaller buildings are set on islands in the lake. The **Eka Karya Botanical Gardens** are an offshoot of the main Botanical Gardens in Bogor (see page 57); watch for the turn-off close to Candikuning (which has a good market). **Bali Handara Kosaido Country Club** has a championship 18-hole golf course ranked among the world's top 50.

Return from Bratan to the south coast on the road via **Pupuan** to see clove and vanilla plantations and some of Bali's most immaculate rice terraces.

Batukaru

A major temple set in the western part of the central hills, Batukaru is surrounded by forest and emanates an atmosphere of powerful holiness.

Mt Agung

Dominating the east coast, Agung is the island's highest and most revered mountain: a haunt of the gods, and site of **Besakih**, largest and holiest of all Bali's temples. The volcano is currently dormant, but in the last major eruption in 1963, 2000 people died and tens of thousands lost their homes.

Besakih Temple ★★★

Far from the soft beauty of Bali's village temples, Besakih is austere, almost harsh. Built high above the coast, with fantastic views towards Lombok and Mt Rinjani, it is approached via a long flight of stairs dominated by the tall black pagodas of the temple itself.

THE EAST

Historically home to some of the island's most powerful kingdoms, eastern Bali probably has more important temples and palaces than any other part.

Start exploring at **Klungkung**, for 300 years the capital of Bali's most powerful kingdom, **Gelgel**, now a slightly frantic junction town, but distinguished by the ornate Balinese architecture fronting the shop-house. **Kerta Gosa**, the Hall of Justice, is on many tour itineraries so can get busy. The open pavilion has a painted ceiling depicting sinners being tortured by demons on the lower levels while the innocent enjoy the pleasures of heaven above. A few metres away is the **Bale Kambang**, the Raja's floating pavilion.

Goa Lawah (20min from Klungkung) is one of Bali's nine most sacred temples, a cave fronted by a shrine 'guarded' by thousands of twittering bats. The temple was renovated in 2007 and is now a very large complex.

Padang Bai

Chiefly known as the ferry port for Lombok, Padang Bai is now developing a tourism industry in its own right. There are small bays and beaches on either side of the main ferry port bay, such as the pretty Blue Lagoon bay, which just has room for two small cafes renting out sunbeds and snorkelling equipment. Above it is one of the upmarket developments where foreigners buy villas as holiday homes.

Candidasa

In the early 1980s Candidasa was a tiny fishing village with a small temple and lotus pond, a lagoon and a couple of backpackers' hostels. Now, after fast and furious expansion, Candidasa has scores of guesthouses and some smart

Above: *Moody Lake Batur, renowned for its superb views.*

BALI BIRD WALKS

To enjoy the finest scenery in Bali, coupled with an introduction to the birds and butterflies, take one of the Bali Bird Walks (every Tuesday, Friday, Saturday and Sunday) from Campuhan, Ubud. Led either by the classically eccentric Englishman Victor Mason or the knowledgable and lively Su, young coconuts consumed en route and lunch at the renowned Murni's Warung are included. Tel: (0361) 975 009, email: su_birdwalk@yahoo.com.

ROUTE PLANNING

Two main routes go through the mountains, one passing Lake Bratan and the other Lake Batur. A popular round trip is:
● drive up to Kintamani and Penelokan
● stop off at Lake Batur
● continue to Bali's north coast
● double back into the mountains near Singaraja
● return to the south coast via Lake Bratan
It is just possible to do this in a day, but staying overnight at Lovina, Tirtagangga or Bratan is much pleasanter.

hotels. In place of peace and simplicity Candidasa has good facilities – from car-hire and money-changing to a good choice of restaurants. The temple is still there, and so is the lagoon, while over the headland you can catch magical tropical sunsets.

Around Candidasa

Tenganan is, like Trunyan, a Bali Aga village and can get very busy. Unlike Trunyan, however, the villagers are quite friendly. Tenganan, still partly fortified, is famous for its rituals and ceremonies and for its unique *grinsing* weaving. As a result of tourist interest and a tenacious adherence to its traditions, Tenganan is a strong and wealthy community.

Amlapura, on the eastern tip of Bali and an easy outing from Candidasa, is the site of an ancient kingdom with not one but three palaces. Puri Kanginan is the largest, but much more beautiful are the water palaces built in the 20th century by the last Raja of Karangasem. At the village of Ujung are the remains of his first project, a small lake surrounded by pavilions representing the sun and moon. Better still is the Tirta Gangga water-palace, a 30-minute drive north of Amlapura. Surrounded by some of the most incredible rice terraces in Bali, it's a wonderful place to stay for a couple of days.

THE NORTH

With mainly black sand beaches and a drier climate, Bali's north coast became popular with tourists much later than the south. The area fell to the Dutch almost 60 years earlier than the south, and, while Balinese Hindu culture survives here, it has been tempered by longer contact with the outside world.

There is an excellent range of accommodation, from upmarket hotels to simple guesthouses where a night's stay costs less than a snack lunch in one of the luxury resorts of Nusa Dua.

The centre of Dutch colonial power in Bali until independence, Singaraja is the biggest town in the north, with two colleges and a library of ancient manuscripts.

Below: *A long-tailed macaque stares back with frank interest from the Balinese forest.*

Lovina Beach and Surrounds ★★

The coastal villages west of Singaraja are known collectively as Lovina Beach. The calm waters make swimming along the reefs, just offshore from the beach, a delight, and an early-morning trip by outrigger canoes, with

the sun rising and the possibility of watching dolphins playing, is unforgettable.

Banjar, Bali's only Buddhist monastery, is up in the hills, just outside the village of **Banjar Tega**. **Sawan**, inland to the east of Singaraja, is a small craft village specializing in gamelan instruments. Off **Tulamben**, at the northern tip of the east coast, is the wreck of a Liberty class ship torpedoed by a Japanese submarine in 1942; now home to reef fish and coral growths, this is one of Bali's most popular dive-sites.

THE WEST

Mountainous, heavily forested and wild, huge areas of western Bali are now within the magnificent **Bali Barat National Park**. This is one of the few parts of Bali where you can still feel like an adventurer, where the local people are surprised – and delighted – to see a Western face. Comprising nearly 80,000ha (176,000 acres) of forest, steep-sided mountain and coral reef, the park is a huge commitment to conservation. One of the world's rarest birds, the brilliant white Bali Starling with dark blue markings, has its home in the lowland forests here. Local legend speaks of lost cities and temples and of the Bali tiger (now extinct). The National Park Office is at **Cekik**, at the junction of the road from Lovina with the road to the ferry port of Gilimanuk. Staff can organize short – or long – jungle treks.

Above: *Mt Batur looms above the lake of the same name, itself formed in an old volcanic caldera.*

PROTECTED REEF

Menjangan Island, reached from Labuhan Lalang, is part of the Bali Barat National Park, and its magnificent coral reefs are protected. The area has Bali's best diving.

RETIREMENT AND SECOND HOMES

Indonesia now offers a year-long retirement visa for people over 55 who wish to spend their declining years (and their foreign exchange) in the country. Second homes can be bought on a lease arrangement. Villas often come complete with plunge pools, sea-views, on-site restaurants and spa services. Check the legalities and rate of return carefully.

Bali at a Glance

By air: Bali's airport, **Ngurah Rai**, is on the coast south of Denpasar just minutes from the main peninsular resorts.

By sea: Ferries from Java arrive at **Gilimanuk** on the far west coast, and from Lombok they dock at Padang Bai. The 4hr ferry ride from Lombok is a pleasant trip, although the hydrofoil to Benoa from Senggigi is much quicker.

Cruising: Several cruise ships operate around Bali and on to other islands, the Lesser Sundas; you can travel on anything from a luxury liner to a converted wooden Bugis sailing ship. For schedules and prices, try www.balicruises.com

Tour operators offer a host of excursions and trips around the island from temple tours to white-water rafting. Even for independent travellers, these are a helpful introduction to Bali. Bali Adventure Tours operates excellent insights into the island through activity holidays. Contact them via www.bali adventuretours.com

Many tourists use the public-transport **minibuses** (*bemos*) which operate all over the island on prescribed routes, while **hire cars** or **jeeps** allow exploration of narrow mountain roads inaccessible to tour coaches. Self-drive is a definite possibility in Bali. When you fill up, make sure the pump meter is at zero, as attendants will try to charge you for fuel you

haven't had. **Motorcycles** can be hired in Kuta and Legian – but check your insurance policy. An International Driving Licence is necessary to hire either a car or a motorbike.

There is accommodation to suit all tastes and purses in Bali, including some of the best hotels in the world. The website baliblog.com (written by local expatriates) has useful tips.

Sanur and *Nusa Dua*
Sanur Beach Hotel, tel: (0361) 288 011, www.aerowisata.com
Respati Bali, Jl Danau Tamblingan 33, Sanur, tel: (0361) 288 427, fax: (0361) 288 046. Mid-range.
Amanusa, Nusa Dua, tel: (0361) 772 333, fax: (0361) 772 335. Expensive and upmarket, as with all Aman hotels.
Ayodya Resort, Jl Pantai Mengiat, Nusa Dua, tel: (0361) 771 102, www.ayodyaresort-bali.com
Melia Bali, Nusa Dua, tel: (0361) 771 510, fax: (0361) 771 360.

Legian and Surroundings
Bali Padma, Legian, tel: (0361) 752 111, fax: (0361) 752 140.
The Kayana, Jl. Raya Petitenget, Kerobokan Kelod, Kuta Utara, tel. (0361) 8476628, www.thekayana.com.
Villa de daun, Jl. Raya Legian, tel: (0361) 756276, www.villadedaun.com
The Semaya, Jl. Laksmana, Seminyak, tel: (0361) 731149,

fax: (021) 731203, www.thesamayabali.com Luxury beachside villas with spa.
Hotel Tugu Bali, Jl. Pantai Batu Bolong, Canggu Beach, tel: (0361) 731701, fax: (0361) 731708, www.tuguhotels.com Fabulous private villas and spa set in lush gardens.
Bali Sandy Cottage, Poppies Gang 2, Kuta, tel: (0361) 753 344, www.balisandy.com Pleasant surroundings. Good value.

There are hundreds of small hotels and guesthouses along the Kuta/Legian strip. Many are excellent value, but few are on the beach.

Tuban
Bali Dynasty, Jl Kartika Plaza, tel: (0361) 752 403, fax: (0361) 752 402.
Sandi Phala, Jl Wana Segara, off Dewi Sartika, tel: (0361) 753 780, fax: (0361) 236 021.
Puspa Ayu Hotel, Gang Puspa Ayu, tel: (0341) 756 721. A good budget option.

Jimbaran
Four Seasons Resort, tel: (0361) 701 010, fax: (0361) 701 020.
Pansea Puri Bali, tel: (0361) 701 605, fax: (0361) 701 320.
Udayana Ecolodge, tel: (0361) 747 4204. An eco-friendly hotel on the hill above Jimbaran Bay.

Batukaru
Sarinbuana Lodge, tel: (0361) 743 5198, www.baliecolodge.com Cottages on the edge of rainforest.

Bali at a Glance

Ubud

Komaneka Resort, Monkey Forest Road, tel: (0361) 976 090, fax: (0361) 977 140.
Ubud Village Hotel, Monkey Forest Road, tel: (0361) 975 571, fax: (0361) 975 069.
The Ina Inn, Jl. Bisma, tel. (0361) 971 093 is good value, just 5-min walk from the main street.
Ubud Hanging Gardens, in Desa Buahan, has luxury villas, tel: (0361) 982 700, www.ubudhanginggardens.com
The Waka Namya Resort, tel: (0361) 975 719, www.wakanamya.com Particularly welcomes children.

Lake Bratan

Bedugul has small hotels and guesthouses around the lake – e.g. the **Bedugul Hotel** and the **Lila Graha**. To get the feel of the hills and experience village life in a degree of comfort, go to **Puri Lumbung**, in Munduk village, tel: (0362) 92810, fax: (0362) 92514, www.purilumbung.com All kinds of activities, from Balinese massage to trekking can be arranged from here.

Candidasa

The Water-Garden (Hotel Taman Air), Jl Candidasa Raya, tel: (0363) 41540, fax: (0363) 41164. Centrally located, with pretty gardens.
Asmara, Jl Candidasa Raya, tel: (0363) 41929, fax: (0361) 775439. Also does diving.
Kubu Bali, tel: (0363) 41532, fax: (0363) 41531.

Lovina Beach

Sol Lovina, Jl Raya Lovina Beach, tel: (0362) 41775, fax: (0362) 41659.
Hotel Banyualit, tel: (0362) 41789, fax: (0362) 41563.
Hotel Celuk Agung, at Banyalit, tel: (0362) 41039, fax: (0362) 41379.
Melka Excelsior, Jl Raya Kalibukbuk, Lovina, tel: (0362) 41552, www.melkaresort.com

West Bali

There are several boutique resorts near the Bali Barat National Park, which offers the best diving in Bali around Menjangan Island. **Mimpi Menjangan Resort**, e-mail: mimpimenjangan@indo.com
Waka Shorea, www.wakashorea.com This has sister outfits dotted around Bali, which emphasize their cultural and environmental authenticity: www.wakaexperience.com

Most hotels have restaurants, and in **Sanur** and **Nusa Dua** there are few good restaurants unattached to hotels. Even so, do try eating out of the hotel for more authentic cooking – and much lower prices. **Kuta** has an excellent range, like the long-established Poppies, tel: (0361) 751 059 (Poppies Lane) and nearby Uns, serving good food in a quieter atmosphere, tel: (0361) 752 607, while TJs serves top-quality Mexican food, tel: (0361) 751 093. Kuta Puri, Poppies Gang 1, Kuta, tel: (0361) 751 903, is typical of the best of the Kuta restaurants: superb cocktails, wonderful ambience, efficient service and tasty food. There are plenty of night-spots in Kuta/Legian: the **Skygarden** is good – try to get a spot on the top floor.
At Sanur, try **The Gangsa**, away from the main street at Jl Tirta Akasa 28, tel: (0361) 270 260.
Ubud has good restaurants – choose the more expensive ones for the best quality food. The Café Lotus, in the centre of Ubud, has good food and décor – and a fine temple on the other side of the lotus pond. Murni's Warung, just before Campuhan bridge, has been serving excellent cakes and meals for years, tel: 975 233. The **Dragonfly**, between Monkey Forest Road and Hanuman Road, offers good food with free wifi access.

Bali has excellent shopping: a lot of Western designers work from here. For clothes head for Kuta, Legian and Ubud. For crafts, buy at source in the craft villages where possible. Visit the government-run **Sanggraha Kriya Asta Handicrafts Centre** in Denpasar (fixed prices, good quality) to get an idea of what the price should be elsewhere. Ubud and surrounding villages are packed with art galleries, ranging from the catchpenny to the stylish. The huge **Agung Rai** complex in Peliatan is one of the best.
To find out what's going on during your stay in Bali, try www.bali-sanurvillage.com

6
Nusa Tenggara

Drier, wilder and less fertile than Bali, the Nusa Tenggara islands are mountainous, sheltering villages and cultures cocooned against change by the poor quality or absence of roads. While cloves and nutmeg drew the colonial powers to Maluku, in the Lesser Sundas they came for the great stands of aromatic sandalwood on Sumba and Timor. The Portuguese had by the 16th century established missions in eastern Flores and the Alor and Solor islands, and continued to hold East Timor long after they lost control of Maluku.

The Dutch paid little attention to the area; not until the 20th century did they move to stamp out headhunting, human sacrifice and intertribal wars. Even then, with no obvious mineral wealth or precious spices, the islands were left almost untouched, particularly their inaccessible interiors. As a result they boast a stunning cultural inheritance.

It is not just the opportunity to observe unique cultures in mountain strongholds that draws visitors. Off the coasts, notably around Flores and Komodo, are fine coral reefs, while the 'dragons' of Komodo Island, the high peak of Gunung Rinjani, and the coloured lakes of Keli Mutu are the focus of national parks. Added mystique was sparked with the 2003 discovery, in a cave in Flores, of the bones of a tiny hominid thought to have lived on the islands up to 12,000 years ago. Since the discovery, scientific argument has raged as to whether the bones represent a completely new species or merely the ancestors of a pygmy race of humans still found on Flores.

CLIMATE

If you travel to Nusa Tenggara during the wet season, Nov– Jun, be prepared for torrential rains to cause flooding and wash away roads – at other times the land will be parched and dry. In some parts of Nusa Tenggara, notably Timor, there can be tropical cyclones. Aug and Sep are generally the driest months.

Opposite: *Pulau Rakit, in Sumbawa's Saleh Bay.*

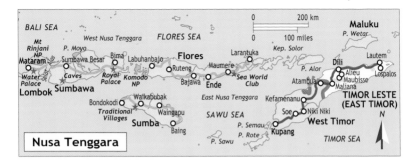

Nusa Tenggara

Outside Lombok, tourism is fairly undeveloped: hotels are simple and roads can be appalling. Administratively, the area is divided into two provinces: the western islands are Nusa Tenggara Barat (NTB) and the eastern ones are Nusa Tenggara Timur (NTT). The eastern part of Timor Island is now the independent country of Timor Leste (formerly East Timor).

LOMBOK

Dominated by the huge, looming bulk of 3726m (12,225ft) Mt Rinjani, Lombok (the name means 'chilli pepper' in Javanese) has a totally different feel to Bali, across the deep Lombok Straits. Lombok is wilder and emptier, drier and less fertile – especially in the south. Around a tenth of the population of 3 million are of Balinese Hindu descent, and you can find rice terraces as finely sculpted as in Bali, ornate Hindu temples and shrines and many Balinese rituals. But Lombok boasts its own special character and identity, not least because the form of Islam practised by its native Sasak people is a unique variant known as Waktu Telu, which is influenced by both animism and Balinese Hinduism.

Ampenan, Mataram, Cakranegara

The four towns of Ampenan, Mataram and Cakranegara and Sweta have expanded and merged to form a single metropolis. It is hectic here, but worth a morning's exploration. At the mouth of the Jankok River, hundreds of outrigger canoes are lined up on the beach. Handmade pottery made by women from all over Lombok is on sale at the Lombok Pottery Centre on Jl Sriwijaya (*see* www.lombokpottery.com) The main market (look for weaving and pottery) is on the road heading north to Senggigi, while a little further on is Sudirman's Antiques, where traditional crafts from all over the island can be found. The Pura Segara temple is a few minutes' walk. The Chinese cemetery beyond has graves highly decorated with coloured porcelain. Many of the dead here were killed in the aftermath of the 1965 attempted coup.

The Nusa Tenggara Barat Museum on Jl Panji Tilar Negara, in Mataram, is worth visiting.

Cakranegara (known as Cakra) is the most rewarding area of the city. A craft and weaving centre, it also boasts two of the most important Balinese buildings on Lombok – the Mayura Water Palace and Pura Meru. Next door to the bus station at Sweta is a vast covered market – the largest and most comprehensive on Lombok.

Mayura Water Palace ★★★

A peaceful oasis amid busy Cakra, the complex centres on a huge, rectangular pond almost covered with lotus flowers. In the middle is the floating palace, the Bale Kambang, a pavilion from which justice was administered in the 18th century. The palace was not always peaceful. In 1894

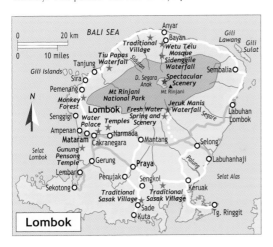

Lombok

FESTIVALS

Like their neighbours across the Lombok Straits, the Balinese of Lombok hold many temple festivals, notably around Cakra. The **Sasak** and **Waktu Telu** ceremonies are mainly in the months just before the rains come – Oct–Nov. If in the area, don't miss the **Nyale** (sea-worm) festival at Kuta, usually in the first or second week of Feb. At full moon ceremonies are often held around Anak Segara lake on Mt Rinjani. There are also spectacular festivities surrounding ceremonies such as circumcision or the opening of a new paddy field.

SENGGIGI BEACH

Twenty-five years ago a visit to Senggigi would have revealed a couple of reasonable hotels and a few guesthouses overlooking beautiful bays. Today there are a dozen star-rated hotels. Nearby, **Batu Bolong** is a Balinese temple on a rocky point from which, it is said, virgins were thrown into the sea. The temple is named for the hole in the rock nearby (*batu* = 'stone', *bolong* = 'hole'). Spend the afternoon on the beach and then watch a technicolor sunset over Bali's Mt Agung. **Pura Segara**, another Balinese temple, is right on the beach to the south of Senggigi, beyond Batu Bolong.

RINJANI NATIONAL PARK

Rinjani's good management was recognized in 2004 when it won a World Legacy Award. Tour operators and most hotels organize treks up Rinjani, as do guesthouses in Ampenan and Cakra. Most people start the trek from Sembalun Lawang village, although there are other entry points too, each with its own cooperative of guides and porters. The trek lasts four days and shouldn't be undertaken lightly – it's cold up there, and it's a tough climb to the top. From the crater rim you see Bali to the west, Sumbawa to the east. the final slog to the peak is tough. Climb down to the huge Anak Segara crater lake (2100m) and bathe your weary limbs in delicious hot springs, coloured milky by minerals. You are unlikely to have the place to yourself – especially at full moon, when both Balinese and Sasak come to make offerings to their ancestors at this sacred place. Find out more at www.lomboksumbawa.com/rinjani

MODESTY

All over Lombok – especially in Kuta – sunbathers should take care to avoid offending Muslim sensibilities. *Never* consider sunbathing topless!

independence fighters here defeated and killed the Dutch General Van Hamm and his entire expeditionary force, which had camped in the palace grounds.

Meru Pura, Lombok's largest and most important Hindu temple, was built in 1720 by Balinese Prince Anak Agung Made Karang to unify the small Hindu kingdoms of Lombok. There are over 30 shrines here.

From the Three Cities

Gunung Pengson is a small Balinese temple complex overlooking the sea on a rocky promontory south of Mataram. Visit early in the morning to see it at its best. Narmada, near Cakra, is the old summer palace of the Raja of Mataram. The lake here was created in 1805, in the shape of Mt Rinjani's Anak Segara lake when the Raja became too old and frail to climb Rinjani itself to make the proper offerings to the volcano's gods.

From Narmada drive to Lingsar, a large temple complex even older (1714) and holier than Pura Meru. Both Sasak Waktu Telu believers and Balinese Hindus worship here, at different shrines. The Waktu Telu shrine includes a spring inhabited by sacred black eels. The village holds and annual dance and music festival, using its important and ancient gamelan. Suranadi, a further 20min into the hills from Lingsar, is a quieter temple and pilgrimage site.

Gili Islands

On the tiny Gili Islands (*gili* means 'island' in the local language) the atmosphere is laid-back and definitely hip. There are lovely beaches here. Gili Meno is the most relaxing and has the fewest tourist facilities. Gili Trawangan has the liveliest atmosphere and the best snorkelling. Gili Air, closest to Lombok, is busy and the most heavily populated. Fourth and quietest is Gili Nanggu, further down the coast near Lembar Harbour. It's best to book travel to the Gilis from Senggigi or even from Bali.

North Lombok

From Pemenang (good market) head north to the stunning white sand beach at Sira, near which are several luxury hotels. There are small fishing villages and dreamy beaches all the way up the coast. From Gondang walk inland to see caves and the Tiu Papas waterfall; a short drive inland is the Waktu Telu village of Gangga. Double back to the coast and continue north to Anyer before reaching Bayan, one of the most important Waktu Telu villages.

South and Central Lombok

Less influenced by the Balinese, the south and centre of Lombok are the heartlands of the island's native Sasak culture. Regular day trips are organized by Senggigi hotels and tour operators, but it is more fun to hire a car or jeep. From the Three Cities take the Praya road. Before reaching busy Praya (good market) turn off to the village of Sukarara, where weavers use wooden backstrap looms to create fine pieces – some taking months to complete. This is now well-established in the tourist circuit, with expensive showrooms – and prices to match.

A few minutes south, take another turning off the main road to visit the pottery centre of Penujak. Other villages in the area also produce traditional pottery. Back on the main road, head south through Sengkol to Sade (also known as Rembitan), a traditional Sasak village where the government has stepped in to protect the traditional thatched houses and rice barns. It feels a bit like a living museum, but it gives a good idea of how people used to live.

From Sade it is a few minutes' drive to Kuta Beach, on the south coast. Still relatively quiet, it is the antithesis of its Balinese namesake. For an in-depth exploration of the area, stay overnight in Kuta; otherwise turn inland via Batu Nampar, making a detour to see the traditional village of Batu Rintang. Then go north through the craft village of Beleka to rejoin the main east–west highway at Kopang.

East Lombok

As you explore the less-visited east, watch for views of Mt Rinjani. North of Labuhan Lombok are fishing villages where foreigners are still a novelty. Offshore from the

Above: *Mt Rinjani, with the Anak Segara crater lake in the foreground.*

ISLAND TIPS

Boats leave from Bangsal harbour for all three main Gilis. In Jul–Aug you need to be on the islands by 10:00 to have a chance of a room.

TRADITIONAL DANCE

While traditional dance features in festivals in country villages – notably Lingsar – it is usually easiest to see dances at performances arranged by tour operators and hotels. Dances include the *tari oncer* drum dance, *batek baris*, *telek* and the *gandrung* love-dance – frowned upon by fundamentalist Muslims. Trance dances are performed in Lombok (as in Java and Bali), but are rarely seen. Javanese *wayang sasak* puppet theatre and *wayang orang* performances are also staged.

small village of Labuhan Pandar (beach bungalows available) are uninhabited Gili Sulat and Gili Petangan, with excellent snorkelling over unspoiled coral reefs.

SUMBA

Western Sumba is most famous for its megaliths and death feasts; eastern Sumba has some of the finest *ikat* weaving in the world. Stylized patterns are used to make pictures of tribal history in vivid, glowing colours. You will see everywhere the small, sturdy horses used in traditional fights (*see* panel on the Pasola).

Waingapu

Administrative capital of the island, the port makes a good centre from which to investigate *ikat* weaving. Head first for Melolo, about an hour's drive from Waingapu. Nearby are several weaving villages. Rende has big slab tombs. At Pau, which has retained a degree of independence and its Raja, ask to see his collection of fabrics. There are more tombs, traditional houses and weaving at Umbara, and Baing is well known for its scarves. At Kailala (just before Baing) the Kailala Beach Resort offers game fishing.

Western Sumba

Celebrated for its Pasola festival, western Sumba is also the place to see death rituals and feasts as spectacular and complex as any in Sulawesi's Toraja. Buffalo, horses and even dogs are slaughtered, and the deceased are buried with their favourite possessions and in rich fabrics they could not have afforded in life. The tomb is marked by massive stones – some weigh many tonnes and require the labour of hundreds to drag them into place. The neat little market town of Waikabubak is the obvious base to explore this area, which is cooler and greener than eastern Sumba.

Villages Near Waikabubak

Pasunga has superb tombs; one, erected in the mid-1920s, required the sacrifice of 150 water-buffaloes. At Anakalang there is a biannual mass marriage. Matakakeri has Sumba's heaviest tomb, at over 70 tonnes. Walk on to

MT TAMBORA

Mt Tambora is the site of the most catastrophic eruption in modern history. It once consisted of two immense peaks over 4000m (13,125ft) high, but in 1815 a series of shattering explosions literally blew the mountain apart. Tens of thousands died during the eruption and in the famines which followed, and the debris created spectacular sunsets and disastrous harvests around the world. Today Tambora consists of a massive crater wall and four young volcanic cones, the highest only 2850m (9350ft). Allow two days to climb the mountain.

Opposite: *A view from Rinca Island, one of the island homes of the famous Komodo dragons.*

an all but deserted hilltop hamlet with yet more tombs. Sodan is the site of a lunar new year ceremony, and boasts a drum covered in human skin. Prai Goli has some of Sumba's oldest megaliths.

SUMBAWA

Surfers have discovered Sumbawa's stunning beaches – notably at Hu'u – and Moyo Island, now partly a game reserve, boasts one of the best hideaway luxury hotels in eastern Indonesia. In the forested hills around Sumbawa Besar are huge neolithic tombs, while the Dou Donggo people of the eastern Sumbawa mountains are known for their animist beliefs.

Sumbawa Besar and Surrounds

Capital of western Sumbawa is Sumbawa Besar ('Big Sumbawa'), a sprawling, noisy Islamic trading centre. The Dalem Loka (Sultan's palace) is worth seeing.

Moyo Island, with its beautiful coral reefs, is easily reached by boat from Sumbawa Besar. Batu Tering (30min drive) has interesting megaliths and stone carvings. Hire a guide to see carved sarcophagi dating back 2000 years.

Bima

Capital of the eastern portion of Sumbawa, Bima lies in a staunchly Islamic area and was formerly an important trading centre. Local women weave colourful chequered sarongs unlike any others in Indonesia, and the market is full of colour.

KOMODO ★★★

Protected by some of the most dangerous waters in Indonesia, the monstrous Komodo dragon (*Varanus komodoensis*), the heaviest lizard in the world, is found only on the islands of Komodo and Rinca. It was formally identified in 1910. An adult can measure over 3m (10ft) long and

---

THE PASOLA

The Pasola, akin to a medieval battle, takes place in four locations in western Sumba. The events involve hundreds of horsemen armed with spears and dressed in traditional costume. Priests await the arrival of the *nyale* sea-worms; once the worms have been examined and the portents inferred, the priests allow the battle, which re-establishes a balance between the upper world and the lower world, to be launched. Traditionally, blood had to be spilled – and it still is, although deaths are less frequent now that sharp-tipped spears have been banned. Pasola battles start usually within a week of the full moon, but the exact date can't be predicted. Feb sees them in the **Kodi area** around Tosi village and around **Sodan**, near **Waikabubak**. In March they move to **Waigalli**, accessible from Waikabubak, and to the area around **Lamboya**. Events are sometimes held at other times of the year – and some tour companies arrange small-scale versions. But to see the real thing, come early and wait for the sea-worms.

weigh over 130kg (290lb), and comes equipped with huge claws and sharp teeth. The dragons hunt deer, wild boar and ponies. They lie in wait, their grey-beige hide perfectly camouflaged by the dry scrub, then lash out at their victim with their muscular tail or sharp teeth. Animals which escape an initial attack seldom survive – the dragon's saliva quickly induces blood poisoning.

The national park is managed as a partnership with local people, the rangers, and an American conservation organization. Accommodation on the island is in lodges at the rangers' camp in a huge and beautiful bay – although the majority of tourists sleep aboard their cruise ships. You will have no difficulty in seeing Komodo dragons around the camp or on ranger-led trips into the bush. Rinca is also a good place to see them, and with fewer tourists. Keep a careful eye open as you look around: the dragons are quite common, but when they sit absolutely motionless they are very hard to spot.

In addition to dragon-watching, you can relax by snorkelling on the reefs in the national park. There are fantastic coral formations and an amazing variety of fish, but take local advice, as the currents are extremely strong.

FEEDING THE DRAGONS

After years of feeding dragons a slaughtered goat when tourists arrived, the authorities now force them to forage for themselves, giving tourists the opportunity of seeing them in more natural surroundings.

CRUISING

Most ship-based tourists only spend a couple of hours on Komodo, but it is rewarding to spend at least a night here and go into the bush when there are fewer people around. Take a ranger – the dragons are dangerous.

FLORES

Named Cabo dos Flores – 'Cape of Flowers' – after the underwater coral gardens by 16th-century Portuguese sandalwood traders, Flores is the most spectacular island in eastern Nusa Tenggara, with wonderful mountainous scenery. Some 375km (235 miles) long and 60km (40 miles) wide, it is surrounded by fine reefs with fantastic diving and snorkelling. The cultures and traditions of Flores' five distinct tribal groups are as varied and interesting as the island's scenery.

Larantuka

Departure point for Alor and Solor, the little port of Larantuka nestles under the flank of the active Ili Mandiri volcano (active). On Good Friday the people of Larantuka parade a statue of Our Lady through the town, led by a religious order known as the Konfrerie. Accompanying songs are in Latin and archaic Portuguese – both now incomprehensible to the people.

Maumere and Surrounds

Maumere is one of the most popular diving spots in Nusa Tenggara, both town and reefs having recovered from a 1992 earthquake. Ladalero, a Catholic seminary high in the hills above Maumere, has wonderful panoramic views of the bay beyond and a justly famous museum. On the south coast (40 minutes' drive), Sikka is probably eastern Flores' best weaving centre.

Moni and Surrounds

Moni is beautifully set in a high valley. Most visitors arrive, stay overnight to see Keli Mutu and then go, but the area is worth a couple of days. Wolowaru has some interesting traditional houses with shaggy, palm-thatched roofs and, inside, carvings. The three most famous weaving villages, Ngella, Wolojita and Jopu, can be visited on foot from Wolowaru in a long day.

Mt Keli Mutu ★★★

High above Moni, the three crater lakes of Keli Mutu are special: each is a different colour, and the colours change from time to time. The two largest are separated by a narrow, rocky spine. The colours in these two are paler than in the third, with yellows, whites, blues, greens and turquoise predominating. The third, 200m (220yd) away, ranges from oily dark green to blood-red and even black.

Bajawa and Surrounds

Ngadhu and *bhaga* structures stand in the squares of the many villages surrounding Bajawa. The *ngadhu* is a carved wooden pole with a rough thatched roof, and symbolizes the male ancestors; the female line is shown in the *bhaga*, a miniature thatched house representing the womb. Bena is

A TERRIFYING RIDE?

Travelling west from Moni to Ende, vertigo sufferers and those of a nervous disposition should sit on the right of the bus. Winding through a spectacular narrow gorge subject to landslides and rockfalls, the road is so narrow that the bus's wheels are almost on the edge of the ravine.

Opposite: *Komodo dragons move sleepily in the dust.*
Below: *The waterfront at Maumere.*

Above: *One of the enchanting traditional dwellings on Flores.*

the best known and best preserved of all the traditional villages in the area. Langa, on the road to Bena, has more *ngadhu* and *bhaga* and some fine weaving. A 20-minute walk towards the rockstrewn slopes of Mt Inieri is a spectacular rift valley. Soa, about 30–40min from Bajawa, is built around a huge, natural amphitheatre with tiers of megaliths.

Riung ★

Take a day trip to this port with its island-studded bay and dazzling reefs. Huge monitor lizards – some almost as large as the Komodo dragons – are found in the area, and at dusk the sky is darkened by flocks of huge fruitbats.

Ruteng

Capital of the Manggarai people, this town is set high on a hillside below an active volcano. The area is famous for *caci* whip-fighting duels. Blood spilled is considered an offering to the ancestor spirits. Duels are a feature of weddings and important ceremonies and a high point of Independence Day (Aug 17) celebrations. Few of the Manggarai's traditional round houses survive, although there are some in Todo, half an hour's drive from Ruteng. The textiles here have brightly coloured patterns embroidered on a black or dark blue background. If you fly over Ruteng, look down from the plane to spot the traditional land-ownership pattern of pie-slice wedges radiating out from a hill-top: that way, everyone got their fair share of hilly and flatter land.

TIMOR

In the more remote hill villages of Timor, people still live in beehive-shaped houses with thatched roofs reaching almost to the ground. Throughout the island you can find heavy woven fabrics featuring geckos, crocodiles and stylized human figures, often in very dramatic colours.

Kupang

Kupang, the main town in West Timor and the provincial capital, is a gateway to Nusa Tenggara and an important entry point from Australia (via Darwin). Visit Teddy's Bar on the waterfront for tours, information and good food.

The regional museum (Museum Negeri) is on Jl Perintis Kemerdekaan. At Oebelo (20 minutes' drive) villagers make and sell traditional stringed instruments. The Savu *ikat* weavers' cooperative (Yasayan le Rai) on Jl Hati Suci is a craft outlet for weavers on remote Savu Island. Weaving can be seen also at Dharma Bakti's factory near the harbour (arrange a visit at their shop at Jl Sumba 32).

Oesao (30min) saw fierce fighting between the Japanese and Australians in 1942, and has a good daily market. There are good beaches (avoid weekends) around the bay. Try Laisana Beach or take a day trip to Semau or Monkey Island. Both have good snorkelling, and there are a couple of small hotels on Semau.

From Kupang

Head inland to Soe (2–3 hours), a cool, dry hill town with a good market and adequate hotels. Hire a car to visit small towns and traditional villages like Boti or Kapan. To the east of Niki Niki (30min) is spectacular countryside with huge rocks (*fatukopa*) said to be a gathering point for the souls of the dead. Atambua is midway between Kupang (7 hours) and Dili in East Timor (6 hours); don't miss the town market for fabrics and jewellery and to see traditional country people.

TIMOR LESTE (EAST TIMOR)

The eastern part of Timor is now an independent country, after being occupied by Indonesia from 1976 to 1999. Tourists were starting to travel here to renew their visa and explore, but in 2007 foreign governments advised avoiding the country because of growing violence between political factions.

Dili, the capital, is an attractive town with old Portuguese buildings and wide, tree-lined avenues. The hill towns of Maubisse and Aileu are centres of coffee-growing – the country's main industry – while around Los Palos are cave paintings and stone sarcophagi. There are wonderful beaches and islands, and people are friendly to foreigners. There is little good accommodation outside Dili.

HAVEN

An early Western visitor to Kupang was Captain William Bligh, who put in here in 1789 after travelling 6500km (4000 miles) in an open boat since being cast adrift by the Bounty mutineers.

ALOR AND SOLOR ARCHIPELAGO

Wild and mountainous, the islands to the east of Flores have barely been affected by the 20th century, let alone the 21st. Animist beliefs, such as the *naga* snake cult persist. Traditional villages drowse beneath smoking volcanoes and fishermen dive for pearls on pristine reefs. The whaling village of **Lamalera** on **Lembata (Lomblen) Island** is the greatest attraction, and on neighbouring **Alor Island** you can see ancient bronze Moko drums whose origins remain a mystery.

Nusa Tenggara at a Glance

GETTING THERE AND AROUND

Cruising: Cruise ships are the most comfortable way to visit and often stop at remote places which are almost impossible to visit any other way.

By air: There is a good network of airports. The three hubs are Denpasar, Bima and Kupang, from where small planes radiate out to remote islands.

By road: Road travel tends to be bumpy. Cars with drivers can be hired in most places.

By sea: Ferries connect the islands. Check locally for up-to-date schedules.

WHERE TO STAY

Lombok

LUXURY

Senggigi Beach Hotel, tel: (0370) 693 210, fax: (0370) 693 339, www.aerowisata.com Includes a selection of luxury villas on-site.

Alang-Alang Boutique Beach Hotel, Jl Raya Mangsit Senggigi, tel: (0370) 693 518, www.alang-beach-villas.com

BUDGET

Lombok Intan Laguna, tel: (0364) 693 090, fax: (0364) 693 185.

Windy Beach Cottages, Pantai Mangsit, tel: (0370) 693 191, fax: (0370) 693 193.

The Gilis

There are dozens of guesthouses on the three main islands. Several dive operators have joined forces to foster reef conservation and run a turtle conservation project.

Narmada

Suranadi Hotel, tel: (0370) 633 686, fax: (0370) 635 630. An old Dutch guesthouse in the hills near the temple – it gets heavily booked at weekends.

Kuta Beach

Coralia Lombok Novotel (www.novotel-lombok.com) is the best, with many other smaller hotels.

Sumba

Nihiwatu Resort, www.nihiwatu.com. An award-winning activity resort with a strong social conscience. On the southwest coast.

Waingapu

Hotel Merlin, Jl Panjaitan, tel: (0387) 61300.

Hotel Sandalwood, Jl Matarwai. Has rooms of variable quality.

Waikabubak

Hotel Manandang, Jl Pemuda 4, tel: (0387) 21297, fax: (0387) 21634.

Mona Lisa Cottages, Jl Adhyaksa, tel: (0387) 21364, fax: (0387) 21042.

Sumbawa

The **Amanwana**, Moyo Island, tel: (0371) 22330, fax: (0371) 22288. A luxury hideaway.

Bima

Lewata Beach, clean, well located (on the road to the airport), pool, good restaurant; **Hotel Parewa**, Jl Soekarno Hatta, tel: (0374) 42652, fax: (0374) 42304.

Sumbawa Besar

Tambora, Jl Kebayan, tel: (0371) 21555.

Tirtasari Cottages, tel: (0371) 21987, 5km (3 miles) out of the town; good restaurant.

Flores

Larantuka

Hotel Fortuna, Jl Diponegoro, just out of town.

Hotel Tresna, Jl Yos Sudarso, more central, and popular with businessmen.

Hotel Rulies, the backpackers' choice – friendly and clean.

Maumere

Sao Wisata Dive Resort, Jl Sawista, Waiara, tel: (0382) 21555, fax: (0382) 21666.

Sea World Club, Maumere 861181, tel: (0382) 21570, fax: (0382) 21102.

Moni

The **Pondok Wisata Arwanty** and the **Watagona Bungalows** have reasonable rooms. The **Sao Ria Wisata** is the most comfortable option but is some way from the village. The **Wisma St Franciskus**, at Detusoko, is plain and clean.

Ende

The following are all reasonable options if you choose the more expensive rooms:

Hotel Dwi Putra, Jl Sudarso, tel: (0381) 21658.

Losmen Ikhlas, Jl A Yani, tel: (0381) 21695.

Hotel Safari, Jl A Yani 65, tel: (0381) 21997.

Bajawa
Hotel Kembang, Jl Martadinata, tel: (0383) 21072. Most upmarket option here, although still basic.
Melati Korina, Jl A Yani 81, tel: (0383) 21162, has reasonable rooms.
Hotel Sunflower, off Jl A Yani, on the outskirts of the village.

Ruteng
Wisma Agung, Jl Waeces 10, tel: (0385) 21080. Pleasantly located amongst rice fields out of the town.
Wisma Dahlia, Jl Bhayang-kari, tel: (0385) 21377. Well-established and with reasonable rooms.
Rima Hotel, Jl A Yani 14, tel: (0385) 22196. Clean, pleasant.

Labuhanbajo
The **Golo Hilltop** has wonderful views, tel: (0385) 41337, www.golohilltop.com The **Bajo Beach Hotel**, Jl Sukarno Hatta, tel: (0385) 41009, and the Matahari, on the same street, are reasonable. There are several hotels on islands a short ride from the mainland: best value is **Seraya Bungalows**, on Seraya Island (tel/fax: (0385) 41258, www.serayaisland.com

Kupang
Hotel Orchid Garden, Jl Gunung Fatuleu, tel/fax: (0380) 833 707. The most upmarket option, with pool.
Hotel Kristal, Jl Tim Tim 59, tel: (0380) 825 100. Also has a swimming pool.

Astiti, Jl Sudirman 146, Kupang, tel: (0380) 21810.

Lombok
Many Balinese souvenirs are made here because labour costs are lower, but there are genuine local crafts too. Look for bamboo and wooden containers, palm-leaf boxes, accessories for betel-chewing, beautiful rough earthenware pottery, rattan basketry, brightly coloured sarongs and scarves (some using *ikat* techniques), musical instruments and replicas of wooden horses used in Sasak ritual dances. In the weaving cooperatives of **Cakranegara** buy fantastic heavy silk or cotton curtaining and upholstery fabrics. Out of town, for weaving try **Sukarara**, **Sengkol**, **Sade** or **Pringgasela** (in east Lombok). **Senanti** and **Sukaraja** specialize in woodcarvings, while **Penujak**, **Banyumuluk** and **Masbagik** are good for pottery. At **Gunung Sari** craftsmen busily make 'antiques' for the art shops.

Sumba
No problem buying fabrics – only in repelling enthusiastic salesmen! You will have read up in advance about what to look for if you are a serious collector – otherwise, as ever, just buy what you like.

Flores
Larantuka
Pearls, woven fabrics; look for old Chinese vases, ceramics.

Maumere
Look for fabrics in the villages or in the market.

Timor
Ikat weavings from all over Nusa Tenggara, sandalwood carvings, betel-nut containers, and weaving/hats made from lontar palm leaves.

Komodo
Many tour operators run trips here, flying into Labuhanbajo or Bima, then by boat to the island. Alternatively, make a day or overnight trip from Labuhanbajo. Find out more at www.komodo nationalpark.org

LOMBOK	J	F	M	A	M	J	J	A	S	O	N	D
AVERAGE TEMP. °F	82	82	82	80	80	82	78	78	80	82	82	82
AVERAGE TEMP. °C	28	28	28	27	27	28	26	26	27	28	28	28
HOURS OF SUN DAILY	9	10	12	13	12	12	13	12	13	13	11	9
RAINFALL in	19	11	6	4	2	3	3	1	1	2	5	10
RAINFALL mm	494	273	148	104	61	73	75	27	18	44	128	245
DAYS OF RAINFALL	22	19	11	8	6	8	4	3	4	4	11	19

7
Sulawesi

The main attractions in Sulawesi (known as the Celebes in colonial times) are the culture of the **Torajan highlanders** in South Sulawesi and the glorious reefs and well-organized diving of the Bunaken Marine National Park in the north.

But Sulawesi has much more to offer, from the boat-building villages of the southern peninsula to the hunter-gatherer tribes of the centre. The road network has improved and inter-island flights make exploration easier, but be prepared for long distances and arduous conditions, especially in mountainous spine and centre of the island.

To the far north are the lands of the **Minahasa**, where Christianity took root with the arrival of the Portuguese. A volcanic region, unlike the rest of Sulawesi, the north boasts stunning coral reefs, colourful dance ceremonies and ancient graves.

Further south, in **Central Sulawesi**, are megaliths, stone statues and huge vats, and the **Lore Lindu National Park**, a mecca for bird-watchers. The southwestern peninsula is dominated by the **Bugis** people, the seafarers who so terrified Western sailors that the word 'bogeyman' came into existence. Traditional Buginese *pinisi* are still constructed in villages along the coast. 4th- and 5th-century Buddhist images have been found in **South Sulawesi**, while Ming and Sung dynasty funerary wares are still occasionally uncovered by archaeologists – and grave-robbers. The Tukang Besi islands, off Southeast Sulawesi, form the **Wakatobi National Park**, with excellent bird-watching and marvellous coral.

CLIMATE

It is rainier in southern Sulawesi than in the north, with microclimates depending on the topography. The Palu valley has the lowest rainfall in Indonesia.

Opposite: The lavishly decorated architecture tells you that you are in Sulawesi's Torajaland.

DON'T MISS

*** Tanah Toraja: Often written just as 'Ta Tor', a beautiful area with the traditional villages of the Toraja people. You have a good chance of being able to attend a Festival of the Dead.
*** Bunaken Marine National Park: Among the best places in the world for scuba diving.
** Tangkoko Batuangus Nature Reserve: Best place to see the tailless Sulawesi macaques (monkeys) and tiny, insectivorous tarsiers.

COURTESY

Makassar is a Muslim city, so dress accordingly – even more so if you visit smaller towns or villages in South Sulawesi. During Ramadan (the fasting month) respect local sensibilities and don't smoke or eat in the street.

Below: *Benteng Ujung Pandang, called by its Dutch builders Fort Rotterdam.*

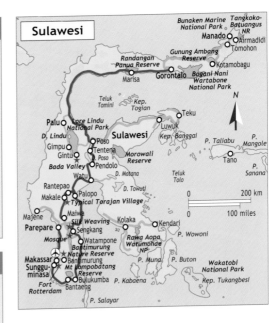

Sulawesi

SOUTH SULAWESI

Gateway to Sulawesi – indeed, to eastern Indonesia – is **Makassar**, where the hair-oil that forced the use of protective antimacassars was made. Known for 40 years after Independence as Ujung Pandang, the city is hot, frenetic and noisy, but has its charms, particularly around the old port area.

The best-preserved ancient fort in Indonesia is **Fort Rotterdam** (Benteng Ujung Pandang). Within the ramparts are two museums, a music and dance conservatory (watch rehearsals) and an archaeological institute.

A ride by *becak* through back streets from a Conrad novel will take you to **Paotere Harbour** to see Buginese schooners or *pinisi*. The **Clara Bundt Orchid Garden** (Jl Mochtar Lufti 15) has some orchids for sale and a great shell collection. Hunt out gold and antique shops in **Jl Somba Opu** – some of which stock early Chinese porcelain (although at high prices). Many of these are attractive fakes, which you may not mind – but you need to know what you are looking for.

Around Makassar

See traditional boatbuilding in villages like **Bantaeng** and **Bulukumba.** At Bira Beach traditional schooners are overhauled, and offer short (3-day) excursions to nearby islands such as Selayar. **Bantimurung**, near the airport, is a nature reserve with waterfalls and many butterflies (very crowded at weekends). Make a combined visit to Bantimurung and **Leang Leang**, which has cave-paintings thousands of years old. There are further caves around **Camba**, a pleasant hill town. **Sungguminasa** – 20–30min south of Makassar – is the site of a former royal palace, now the Ballalompoa Museum housing a huge gold crown and other exhibits. There are some diving at small islands off the coast of Makassar.

The Toraja Road

You can fly in and out of Torajaland from Makassar to avoid the 6-hour drive, but it's better to fly one way and drive the other to see the panoramic mountain scenery. The normal route is via the seaport **Parepare**; rather longer is to go via **Watampone (Bone)**, former capital of South Sulawesi's strongest state, to take in the interesting **Museum Lapawowai** en route.

MAJOR SITES IN TORAJA

Lemo: The most famous *tau tau* site, with rows of wooden statues made to commemorate the dead. Many are now modern replacements, older ones having been stolen for the antiques trade or removed by families for safekeeping. Get there before 09:00 when the *tau tau* go into shadow.

Kete Kesu: Cliff graves, caves and traditional houses. Walk through paddies to Palatokke; return by road to Rantepao.

Londa: Big burial cave with *tau tau* above. Nearby is a tree in which dead babies were lodged, their souls growing with the tree.

Lempo and Nanggala: Traditional houses and rice barns. You pay to take photographs.

Tampangallo (Makale) More *tau tau* and graves.

GUIDES

When hiring a guide, try to make sure you find a local person (Toraja guides should carry identification) rather than enterprising Buginese who won't know the area so well.

Left: *Rice paddies in Torajaland.*

Above: *Sigunta village in Torajaland.*

WALKS AROUND TORAJA

Trekking in Toraja is excellent, partly because of the cooler climate. There are dozens of short walks around the villages and burial sites; a longer walk (4 hours) is from Batutumonga in the hills above Rantepao, downhill all the way to Sadan (or even Rantepao) past traditional houses and cliff graves.

AT THE MARKET

The market takes place in Rantepao every six days. You may be charged a fee to get in, but it is worth it for the dozens of stalls selling all manner of local goods, food and domestic animals – don't miss the pig market! You may even catch a cock-fight. The long bamboo containers hold fermented sugar-palm sap or rice wine – delicious early in the morning, but sour later.

Tanah Toraja ★★★

Tanah Toraja ('Land of the Toraja') is still one of Indonesia's most popular destinations for cultural tours. Tourism has brought prosperity, but development has not marred the beauty of the green river valleys and vast sweeps of rice terraces beneath rocky mountain ridges.

The traditional homes of the Toraja people, *tongkonan*, cluster behind huge stands of bamboo. Houses and rice-barns have upturned roofs like a ship. The walls are beautifully carved and painted with red, yellow, black and white clan motifs. Water-buffalo skulls and horns indicate past ceremonies.

The Dutch won control of Toraja early in the 20th century by bringing warring tribes down from the hills and outlawing human sacrifice. Missionaries followed and the area is now mainly Christian but, as in many parts of Indonesia, traditional beliefs in an afterworld and ancestor-reverence persist.

These beliefs are at their most spectacular in the Torajan Festival of the Dead. Festivals can take years to organize as the dead cannot be consigned to the afterlife until their earthly inheritance is settled between family members – and disputes are common. Before the funeral the body remains at home (wrapped in funeral cloths) and the deceased is not considered to have fully passed on to the next world. The full ceremony takes up to a week. Even a relatively small event may involve killing 30–40 pigs (the meat is later distributed around the village) and a half-dozen water-buffalo. The government now taxes animal offerings and places restrictions on expenditure as events were becoming more and more elaborate. Guests, including tourists, are welcome to attend.

The highlight is the funeral feast, involving animal slaughter (not for the squeamish!). The ceremony culminates in the body being taken to a cliff grave where the soul joins the ancestral spirits. Wealthy families commission a *tau tau*, a wooden statue of the dead person to which their soul can return.

Most visitors stay in **Rantepao**, in the beautiful Sadan River valley. The district capital, **Makale**, a 20-minute drive away, is quieter but less convenient. The area is easy to get around – major sites of interest are signposted – and there are traditional houses, barns and burial sites everywhere. Walk away from paved roads to see untouched villages.

WEST SULAWESI

The new province (since 2004) of West Sulawesi offers rough roads, small towns where tourists never visit, and a Christianised culture similar to Toraja. A three-day hike through the mountains from Mamasa, staying in family homes or small guesthouses, brings you to Toraja – an amazing alternative way to get there.

CENTRAL SULAWESI

Fly into Palu, then travel by road to Kamarora, where the headquarters of the Lore Lindu National Park are located. There is good bird-watching here and some good trekking deeper into the park. For more adventure, travel from Palu to Gimpu (4 hours) and walk along forest trails used by pack-horses to Gintu, in the Bada Valley (3 days), to see the mysterious megalithic statues and a further day's walk to the Besoa Valley, where there are huge stone vats, whose original purpose is unknown. Head for Gintu, in the centre of the park – There is simple accommodation at Kamarora, Gintu and Doda.

The area around Poso and Tentena is out of bounds because of inter-religious fighting.

NORTH SULAWESI

North Sulawesi is one of Indonesia's best areas for general touring because of the well surfaced roads, pretty villages, variety of scenery and attractions, and the friendly people. You can trek in wildlife reserves, see crater lakes and bubbling mudpits, and visit interesting archaeological sites – all surrounded by exquisite scenery. The Minahasa people are among the most prosperous in Indonesia and most are Christian.

WALLACEA

Sulawesi forms part of the biogeographical zone called Wallacea, marking the transition between the fauna and flora of Asia and of Australia. Much of the wildlife is unique to the island, e.g. the anoa, a dwarf buffalo, and the babirusa, like a pig but no relation. There is an astonishing variety of huge butterflies, and bird-watchers flock to view Sulawesi's high number of endemic species.

Below: *An ancient megalith in Central Sulawesi.*

Above: *A Sulawesan pre-Christian tomb, or waruga.*

Manado and Surrounds

Capital of North Sulawesi, Manado is a bustling, efficient seaside city. **Bunaken Marine National Park** is the main draw. A 30-minute boat ride from the mainland are white sand beaches and well protected coral reefs with superlative snorkelling and diving. In the city, check out the **Provincial Museum** (Jl Supratman). Horse- and bullcart-races are occasionally held at **Ranomuut racetrack** east of the city.

Tomohon, a blissfully cool hill town with an interesting market, is a good base for exploring the region. The North Sulawesi peninsula is where two tectonic plates meet, so there is plenty of volcanic activity. **Mount Lokon** is a two-hour climb (easy but hot) from Wailan on the Manado–Tomohon road. The crater lake boils away when activity increases, and occasionally the mountain is 'closed' because of eruptions. A 20-minute drive from Tomohon is **Lake Linau**, a crater lake that changes colour according to the light. There are mud pools and small geysers: stick to the paths or risk being casseroled!

In pre-Christian times people here buried their dead in upright tombs, *warugas*. There are fine examples at **Airmadidi, Sawangan** and **Likupang**, many adorned with carvings revealing how the occupant died. **Batu Pinabetengan** is a huge stone marking the former meeting place of Minahasan chiefs.

Tara Tara village, close to Tomohon, is a centre of Minahasa culture where dance performances are sometimes held. Ask about the *cakalele* war dances, with dancers wearing Portuguese-style helmets and brightly coloured clothes.

Tangkoko Batuangus Nature Reserve

This pleasant reserve (2 hours from Manado) is one of the best places to see Sulawesi's elusive wildlife. Tailless Celebes apes and tiny tarsiers are frequently seen, while the megapode, which buries its eggs for hatching in the hot volcanic sands, takes more persistence to spot. There are black sand beaches and some good lowland forest. Overnight accommodation is in simple hostels. Tours can be arranged in Manado or Bitung.

Sulawesi at a Glance

GETTING THERE AND AROUND

By air: Makassar is the main gateway to Sulawesi with onward flights to cities in other provinces.

By road: Roads between Makassar and Rantepao and around Manado are good. Elsewhere be prepared for a bumpy ride.

WHERE TO STAY

Makassar
Makassar Golden Hotel, Jl Pasar Ikan 50-52, tel: (0411) 333 000, fax: (0411) 320 951, www.makssargolden.com This hotel is situated right on the seafront.
Sahid Jaya Makassar, Jl Dr Sam Ratulangi 33, tel: (0411) 875 757, fax: (0411) 875 858.
Less expensive are the **Losari Beach Hotel**, Jl Penghibur 3, tel: (0411) 326 062, fax: (0411) 313 978, and the **Wisata Inn**, 36-38 Sultan Hasanuddin Street, tel: 324 344, 322 186, fax: 312 783

Toraja
There are dozens of hotels and guesthouses, including:
Hotel Marante, Jl Jurusan Palope, tel: (0423) 21616, fax: (0423) 2122.
Toraja Cottage, tel: (0423) 21475.
Pia's Poppies, Jl Pong Tiku 27, tel: (0423) 21121.
Duta 88, Jl Sawerigading 12, tel: (0423) 23477.
Six kms south of Makale is the Kandora Mountain lodge, an ideal base for trekking. Tel: (0423) 21701, fax: (0423)

27344, kandora@toraja.net

Palu
Hotel Sentral, Jl Kartini 6, tel: (0451) 422 789, fax: (0451) 428 288. Ask for an upstairs room.
Palu Beach Hotel, Jl Raden Saleh 1, tel: (0451) 421126.
Buumi Palupi Hotel, Jl Manunsarkoro 21, tel: (0451) 422513.

Manado
There are several international chain hotels in Manado, including: **Ibis Manado**, tel: (021) 570 6929, fax: (021) 570 8331, and **Novotel Manado**, Jl Sam Ratulangi 22A, tel: (0431) 55555, fax: (0431) 63545.
An hour from Manado, the **Highland Resort Tomohon** offers spa treatments and a peaceful stay in the hills. Tel: (0431) 353333, fax: (0431) 353777.

Bunaken Dive Resorts
These are well-organized, relaxed and good places to stay even if you aren't a diver. The website of the North Sulawesi Watersports Association www.divenorthsulawesi.com lists the resorts.

Southeast Sulawesi
Wakatobi Resort, Kuta Poleng Blok D-1, Jl Setiabudi, Simpang Siur, Kuta, Bali, tel: (0361) 759669, fax: (0361) 752729, www.wakatobi.com There is also a cruise ship, the *Pelagian*, based on the islands (contact details above).

WHERE TO EAT

The seafood in Makassar is excellent, the best in Indonesia. Try grilled fish (*ikan bakar*), crab (*kepiting*) and giant prawns (*udang*). However, avoid *soto makassar*, unless you enjoy buffalo intestines.

SHOPPING

The best crafts are sold in **Makassar** and **Rantepao**. Jl Somba Opu has shops with silver filigree jewellery from Kendari in Southeast Sulawesi and local gold. Also hunt beautiful, brightly coloured silk sarongs, Chinese ceramics and local brasswork. In **Toraja**, buy painted and carved woodwork: boxes for betel nut and tobacco, bamboo water-carriers, and 60cm (2ft) machetes with bone-inlaid ebony handles.

MAKASSAR	J	F	M	A	M	J	J	A	S	O	N	D
AVERAGE TEMP. °F	78	78	78	78	78	78	78	78	80	80	80	78
AVERAGE TEMP. °C	26	26	26	26	26	26	26	26	27	27	27	26
HOURS OF SUN DAILY	6	7	8	10	11	10	12	13	13	12	9	7
RAINFALL in	28	20	15	8	5	2	2	1	1	2	12	22
RAINFALL mm	711	520	375	201	126	57	43	10	29	59	308	566
DAYS OF RAINFALL	25	23	21	18	15	10	7	3	5	9	20	23

8
Maluku

For hundreds of years the world's only source of nutmeg, mace and cloves, the islands of Maluku (the Moluccas) played a formative role in the history of empire-building by European nations. In the centre of the archipelago are the **Bandas**, tiny volcanic islands where nutmeg and its associated mace (the reddish fibres covering the nut) originated. In the north the islands of **Ternate**, **Tidore**, **Bacan** and **Halmahera** are the ancestral home of all the world's clove trees.

For centuries the route to the Spice Islands was guarded by Arab traders. The first Europeans to discover the route were the Portuguese, who sent an expedition to Banda in 1512. The Spanish arrived – with Magellan – a decade later, followed soon after by the English and Dutch.

In the early 17th century the Dutch won control of the islands through one of history's most powerful mercantile organizations, the **Dutch East Indies Company** (VOC). Having captured Portuguese forts in **Ambon** and won control of the island, the VOC murdered competing English merchants. Then in 1621 VOC Governor General Jan Pieterszoon Coen seized control of the Bandas and the nutmeg monopoly. Within weeks about 15,000 Bandanese had been slaughtered. The English were ejected from their last stronghold, the island of **Run** – and compensated with the then insignificant swampy island off the coast of New England, subsequently named Manhattan.

By now Coen and his lieutenants also had effective control of Ternate and Tidore. The cultivation and sale of cloves on these islands was banned, to centralize

CLIMATE

The rainy season in Ambon and southern Maluku is from April to August – the opposite to most of Indonesia – so the best months to visit are between October to January. Rain patterns in northern Maluku are like those of the rest of Indonesia.

Opposite: *Begun in 1611 by the Dutch, Bandaneira's huge Fort Belgica has survived the test of time – and several major earthquakes.*

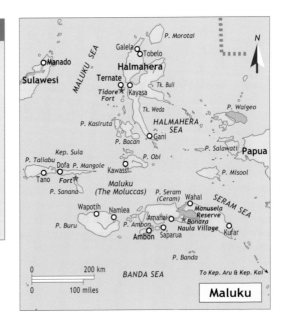

Below: *Drying nutmeg and cloves in the sunshine on Tidore Island.*

production on Ambon and ensure a monopoly. Eventually, however, clove and nutmeg seedlings were smuggled out to be cultivated in other parts of the world, breaking the monopoly and contributing to the demise of the VOC.

Nutmeg and cloves are still harvested here, but it is the islands' stunning natural beauty, world-class diving and turbulent history that draw travellers. History is there to be stumbled over. Innumerable forts crumble under the grip of vines and banyan trees, and cannon embossed with the VOC emblem slowly rust under the tropical sun. The **Aru** archipelago is famous for its birds-of-paradise, while in the forests of **Halmahera** and **Ceram** there are flocks of white cockatoos and brightly coloured parrots – although the illegal trade in birds is fast reducing the population.

Since 1998 there has been conflict between the Christian and Muslim communities in Maluku, with the result that tourists are advised to be cautious about plans to visit the area. Government advice in most tourist-generating countries is against travel to Ambon and some other areas because of continuing violence, including bomb attacks in 2007. The chance of being caught up in any violence is minimal, however, and tourists are returning – for instance the annual Darwin to Ambon Yacht Race recommenced in 2006, and several cruises are offered. The unrest means that there is little tourist infrastructure, although the lack of tourists is a boon in that you would have the islands to yourself apart from a few other hardy adventurers.

AMBON

Arrival at Ambon, the best-known of the Maluku islands, is spectacular. Planes fly in low over ancient volcanoes before a final approach over Ambon harbour. The airport is a 30–40min taxi ride from town, skirting the sea most of the way, or as a pleasant alternative you can cross the bay by ferry.

Ambon Town

Ambon Town is the administrative and business hub of Maluku. If you are spending a day or two here, **Siwalima Museum** offers a good introduction to the history and culture of Maluku.

The huge **Pattimura monument** commemorates one of Indonesia's early independence fighters, born in neighbouring Saparua; more impressive and with good views is the **monument to Martha Christina Tiahahu,** also a freedom fighter. If you are in the area at the right time (May 14–15) don't miss the **Pattimura Day** events.

Outside Ambon Town

Just outside town is a beautifully maintained **World War II cemetery**. **Waai** has an underground sacred spring, home to huge, semi-tame eels and carp fed by shrine priests. Nearby **Honimua** is a departure point for ferries to Seram and to pretty Pombo Island. **Soya Atas**, easily reached in the hills above Ambon, has interesting megaliths and sacred standing stones, an old church and a stone water container which – according to local legends – never runs dry.

SPENDING MONEY

Change travellers' cheques at banks on Ambon and Ternate or use ATMs. Carry plenty of rupiah with you, especially smaller denominations, as these are hard to come by in more remote destinations.

TUAK

The mildly alcoholic fermented sap of various palm trees is sweet and refreshing in the morning but bitter in the afternoon.

CHANGING TIMES

Intercommunal violence in Maluku since 1998 has complex roots. It is partly because Suharto's removal in 1998 allowed long-suppressed tensions to reveal themselves, including the antipathy between the large numbers of Muslim settlers and the native Christian population.

At **Hila** (about an hour's drive) is a church dating from 1780 and the 16th-century **Mapauwe Mosque**. Nearby is majestic **Fort Amsterdam**, and along the coast are more, smaller, forts. Further away, the **Hitu Peninsula** is a Muslim stronghold. At **Mamala** village the annual *sapulidi* ritual is held shortly after the end of Ramadan: village youths beat each other bloody, but an hour later no mark remains.

There is good diving at several locations within half an hour of Ambon: the best way to see these is to take a dedicated tour on a live-aboard dive boat.

Banda Islands

People visit the Banda islands for a short trip and end up spending days just wandering around, lost in the crumbling echoes of the islands' dramatic past as a centre of world commerce. Visit Fort Belgica on Banda Neira and the old churches with their gravestones of long-dead Europeans. The seascapes and sunsets are marvellous, and the snorkelling is magnificent.

Kai Islands

A few hardy backpackers and birdwatchers visit these islands. Tual (on Dulah/Kai Kecil) is the capital of South-east Maluku – but don't expect anything sophisticated! There are fabulous beaches such as Pasir Panjang (15 km/9 miles From Tual).

NORTH MALUKU

Like Ambon and Banda to the south, the islands of this chain are littered with ancient forts.

Ternate

The island's capital is **Ternate City**, sprawling along the narrow coastal plain. You can walk from one end of the town to the other in an hour. **Fort Oranje** was built by the Dutch in 1637, and has several old cannon inscribed with the VOC seal. Islam came to Ternate early, and the **Great Mosque** is worth a visit.

The **Kedaton** is still the home of the Sultan of Ternate, and part of it is open to the public; the colours of the palace servants' turbans signify their rank. Offerings are made to the palace spirits three times weekly. The **Crown of Ternate**, credited (like the Sultan) with supernatural powers, is not on public show. The museum has an eclectic collection of exhibits, but opening hours are erratic. Nearby, the huge dark covered market is worth a visit.

Around the Island

Ternate is one vast volcano rising to the smoking peak of **Mt Gamalama** (1721m; 5646ft) – a fantastic but tough climb through blasted lava fields. The lower slopes are a green sea of clove trees. Nutmeg is also grown here.

A short walk to the west of town is **Fort Kayuh Merah** ('red wood'); here sunset offers beautiful views towards Tidore and Maiara. The lovely **Danau Laguna**, its surface covered by lotus flowers, is said to be inhabited by a sacred crocodile. The road goes straight through the remains of 16th-century Portuguese **Benteng Kastella**. Beyond, **Sulamadeha** has a black sand beach with safe swimming (crowded at weekends). Take a motorboat to **Hiri Island** (10min), where there is good snorkelling and legends of a visiting mermaid. At **Batu Angus** ('burned rock') are spectacular remains of 18th-century lava flows.

Left: *On the south of Ternate City, the unfinished Benteng Kayu Merah was built in 1510 by the Portuguese.*

Right: *The view up to Mt Gamalama in the centre of Ternate Island.*

Tidore and Halmahera

A beautiful 45min boat ride from Ternate's Bastiong Harbour, the 'capital' of Tidore – **Soa Siu** – is no more than a village. Fewer relics survive here than on Ternate, although there is an old fort above Soa Siu and another near **Rum**, the arrival point from Ternate. **Halmahera**, the largest island in North Maluku, was once the clove sultanate of Gilolo. Little remains of Halmahera's past; most visitors are ornithologists or anthropologists. Halmahera is currently only accessible by boat. The highest point on the island is Mt Gamkonora (1635m; 5364ft), which had a major eruption in July 2007.

At **Kao Bay** see the wreckage of Japanese vessels bombed during an epic World War II battle. **Tobelo** is a trading port with one of the best traditional markets in Maluku; the town is the largest on Halmahera. Around **Galela** (the northeasatern part of thte island) are pristine white sand beaches, more volcanoes and the beautiful Lake Galela. The birdlife is fantastic, with many hornbills, cockatoos and parrots.

Maluku at a Glance

By air: **Ambon** is the main gateway to the region: there are daily flights from Jakarta via Makasar in South Sulawesi, and from Manado in North Sulawesi. There are also services from Ambon to **Tual** in the Kai Islands and then on to **Tanimbar**. There are currently very few flights between Ambon and **Banda**. Leave yourself a spare day when returning to Ambon from any of the smaller islands.

By road: Roads in Ambon, Saparua and Ternate are surprisingly good. Elsewhere be prepared for unsurfaced roads and makeshift bridges. There are virtually no roads (or cars) in the Banda Islands. Much inter-island travel throughout Maluku and coastal areas of Papua is accomplished by motorized canoes called 'johnsons' (after the principal make of outboard motor). They run regular routes between coastal settlements, or they can be hired; private hire is expensive.

Cruising: Several cruise ships and live-aboard dive boats still operate around the Maluku islands, mostly operating out of Bali. Contact www.song linecruises.com or www. archipelago-fleet.com for schedules etc.

By sea: Taking a passenger ferry between the islands is a good way to experience Indonesian culture (book the best cabin you can afford). *See* www.pelni.co.id for schedules (in Indonesian).

Outside Ambon, Banda and Saparua there are no tourist-class hotels. There are basic lodgings on Seram and Buru. Expect to eat fish, fish and more fish.

Ambon
Hotel Amboina, Jl. Kapitan Ulupaha, tel: (0911) 341725.
Hotel Tirta Kencana, Jl. Raya Amahusa, tel: (0911) 351867. By the beach, good service.
Halim's Restaurant, on Jl. Sultan Hairun, good meals.

Banda
Hotel Delfika, tel: 0910 21027, is good, though simple. There are no restaurants.

Kai Islands
There are small guesthouses in Tual, and beach cottages at Pasir Panjang.

The easiest way to visit Maluku is to join a tour, especially a cruise ship or live-aboard dive boat. Contact Maluku Divers at Jl Aman Lamte, Latulahat, tel: (0911) 323216, fax: (0911) 323909, www.@unexplore dadventures.com for the latest tour details and an update on the security situation in Ambon. This is a company with a strong 'helping the community' ethic.

There is good diving throughout Maluku, although some reefs have been destroyed by blast-fishing. The best option remains to follow the programmes of live-aboard dive boats or dive resorts.

Most beaches on Ternate and Tidore are of black volcanic sand. Beaches in northern Halmahera, around Galela and on the islands in the Bay of Tobelo are pearly white and dreamlike; for sheer beauty the Kai Islands win hands down.

The best handicrafts are to be found in **Ambon**: intricate ships made from cloves, mother-of-pearl collages, weavings and primitive carvings from **Tanimbar** and **Wetar**. Woven baskets can be bought in markets on all the islands, with pottery in **Kai Besar** and the **Lease Islands**.

AMBON	J	F	M	A	M	J	J	A	S	O	N	D
AVERAGE TEMP. °F	82	82	82	80	80	78	78	78	78	80	82	82
AVERAGE TEMP. °C	28	28	28	27	27	26	26	26	26	27	28	28
HOURS OF SUN DAILY	7	7	8	6	6	4	4	4	5	7	8	7
RAINFALL in	5	5	5	11	20	25	24	16	9	6	4	5
RAINFALL mm	127	119	135	279	516	638	602	401	241	155	114	132
DAYS OF RAINFALL	12	13	13	12	19	21	22	21	16	10	10	13

9
Papua

Indonesia's final frontier and one of the last great wild places in the world, Papua (formerly Irian Jaya) is the western half of New Guinea, a land of snow-topped mountains and huge swamps, of dry savannas and dense jungles where kangaroos clamber through the trees and birds-of-paradise conduct ritual dances. Off the north coast are fine coral reefs and beaches, while inland, in national parks like Lorentz – topped by the massive Puncak Jaya – and Wasur, are birds and other animals found nowhere else in the world.

Anthropologists estimate there are at least 250 different tribal groups in Papua, including the Dani of the Baliem Highlands and the Asmat, famous for their carvings.

Papua's people are Melanesian and, despite the influx of settlers from overcrowded Java and the influence of missionaries and teachers, many Papuan tribes hold to their traditional lifestyles. By far the most serious current threat to both people and wildlife is the virtually uncontrolled plunder of seas, forests and minerals by mulitnational companies.

BIAK AND SURROUNDS

Biak, off the northwest coast, is a refuelling point for flights from the USA and a good entry point to Papua, with great island-hopping possibilities. But don't expect a tiny, sleepy village: Biak is a major Indonesian naval base and a centre for the fish trade, including tuna-processing and oyster-beds.

Reefs around Biak are as rich as anywhere in the world, with many still virtually untouched. Avoid the rainy months

CLIMATE

Plan visits to the **Jayapura area** from Apr–Sep, when it is less likely to be rainy. The **Central Highlands** are cool all year round, with frequent rain. The **south coast** is coolest from Jun–Sep and wettest from Jan–May.

Opposite: *A typical Dani compound in the upper Baliem Valley.*

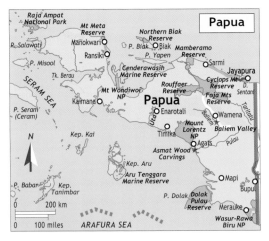

of Aug–Oct when surface run-off lowers visibility.

Elements of cargo cults survive in remote villages, along with a tradition of firewalking. Several of the smaller islands are nature reserves, but don't expect any tourism infrastructure – come equipped with a sense of adventure. The area has everything the intrepid traveller dreams of … except air-conditioning and smart restaurants.

Bosnik (18km/11 miles east of Biak town) has a white sand beach and views to the Padaido Islands. Charter an outrigger canoe to the islands for wonderful snorkelling. En route to Bosnik, stop off at Telaga Biru, a beautiful blue lagoon. Near Bosnik is a bird park with birds-of-paradise and other rare species.

Korem is a bumpy 1-hour journey to the island's north coast through jungles and mountains. Pearl-fishers operate in Korem Bay, while in the hills above are caves used by the Japanese during World War II. Supiori Island, which can be reached by road and ferry by the determined, is a nature reserve – lots of parrots and cockatoos and fine off-shore reefs.

THE NORTH COAST
Jayapura

Jayapura is the gateway to and administrative capital for Papua, which is now divided into two provinces. There are flights to all main points in Papua from here, and (compulsory) police travel permits (*surat jalan*) can be arranged for trips to the interior.

Museum Negeri (Jl Raya Sentani in Waena suburb) has traditional weapons, shell money, looms and stuffed birds-of-paradise. The museum shop sells a small range of handicrafts.

DON'T MISS

★★ **Biak**: also called Kota Karang – meaning 'City of Coral' – with unspoilt off-shore reefs to which divers come from the world over.
★★★ **The Highlands**: home of the fascinating Dani people and dozens of other tribes.

Below: *A spotted cuscus in the Jayapura region.*

Around Jayapura

Abepura – home of Cendrawasih University – is 15 minutes from Jayapura on the airport road. Visit (mornings) to see the university museum (Jayapura Museum), with its wonderful carvings and musical instruments – the most comprehensive collection of Papuan arts in one place.

The small village of Hamadi saw the Allied landing in 1944. A couple of rusting tanks still sit on nearby beaches. MacArthur's campaign HQ was at nearby Base G, now the Tanjung Ria Beach Resort, with good water-sports facilities. 'Asmat carvings' on sale here are actually made in nearby Sentani. Above the city is 'Skyline Hill', with beautiful views of the bay; Hindu and Buddhist temples are situated here.

Near the airport, Sentani is very relaxed with a range of small hotels and guesthouses, although the mosquitoes are particularly hungry here. Climb the hill at Doyo Lama (10min drive southwest of Sentanie) to see an odd group of over 70 standing stones, some engraved with human figures, or Mt Ifar to the northeast to visit the MacArthur Monument. Lake Sentani has fishing and weaving villages on stilts around its shore. Hunt out local carvings and pottery during a motorized canoe ride on the lake.

Above: *Lake Sentani, with its scattering of small volcanic islands.*

THE SOUTH COAST
The Asmat Region

Home of the once notorious Asmat tribe, once notorious cannibals, much of the southern coast of Papua is threatened by ecological disaster through uncontrolled logging, while inland the Freeport McMoran mine is devastating huge swathes of the Sudirman mountain range to collect copper, gold and silver. Access is via Agats, a small town connected by wooden boardwalks across the swamps, with a world-class museum of carvings and other local artefacts. Only plan river trips into the interior if you have time, money and patience. This is the place for genuine Asmat art – local Catholic priests have been working with carvers for years. Buy fantastic pieces for a fraction the price you would pay in Bali.

THE INTERIOR

Travel in the interior has loosened since the Indonesian government allowed provinces more autonomy after 2001. However, expect very basic travel facilities – come armed with mosquito repellent and a strong sense of adventure!

Wasur National Park

Here a wide selection of Papuan wildlife can be seen quite easily. Kangaroo, deer and wild pigs roam across the swampy savanna, while an excellent variety of birdlife can be spotted in the open eucalyptus forests and coastal woodland. The park is only a 30-minute drive from the town of Merauke, and there are several small guesthouses in the villages.

The Highlands ★★★

The Dani of the Baliem Valley (known to the outside world only in 1938) are the best-known of dozens of tribes in the high mountains of central Papua. Most men wear nothing but a penis gourd (*koteka*), despite the bitter cold of the highland nights, while women wear grass skirts and carry orchid-fibre string bags on head-straps. The fields are still worked with stone tools. Tribal warfare continues. If your guide changes your trekking route and won't say why, possibly two tribes are in bloody dispute on the path ahead.

Wamena and the Baliem Valley

A 50-minute flight from Jayapura, Wamena sits over 1600m (5250ft) above sea-level in the high, wide Baliem Valley. It consists mostly of government and missionary offices with a handful of small hotels and shops. Although it is the major tourist destination in Papua, even at peak season the area is not busy.

The market is the focal point, patronized by Dani tribesmen (complete with *koteka*) and enterprising traders from the coast and beyond. The Dani live in round, thatched houses in fenced compounds. Villages close to Wamena have become commercialized, especially Akima (Momi) with its infamous smoked mummy of a former tribal leader. (Other villages with smoked ancestors on display are Jiwika, Kimbim Pommo and Wasalma.)

Below: *Young Dani men in traditional costume.*

Papua at a Glance

By air: Fly to **Biak** or **Jayapura** from Jakarta, Makasar or Bali, or from Papua New Guinea. Jayapura is a full day's journey and two time zones from Jakarta. Centres served from Jayapura and Biak include **Wamena**, **Agats** and **Merauke**. Always reconfirm your departure upon arrival.

Biak
Hotel Irian, Jl Moh. Yamin, tel: (0981) 21939. A historic hotel, opposite the airport.
Nirmala Beach Hotel, Jl Sorido Raya 26, Kampung Samau, tel: (0981) 26333.
Hotel Arumbai, Jl Selat Makassar 3, tel: (0981) 21835, www.arumbaihotel.com

Jayapura
Swiss Belhotel, tel: (0967) 551888, email: jayapura@ swiss-belhotel.com. Jayapura's only 4-star hotel.
Hotel Yasmin, Jl Percetakan 8, tel: (0967) 533 222.
Hotel Matoa International, Jl. Jend A Yani 14, tel: (0967) 531065, fax: (0967) 531437
Hotel Dafonsoro, Jl. Percetekan Negara 21-24, tel: (0967) 531676. Has a good Indonesian restaurant.

Sentani
Hotel Carfin, Jl Flafon, tel: (0967) 591 478, is near the airport and clean.
Hotel Sentani Indah, Jl Raya Hawaii, tel: (0967) 591 900, has a pool.

Hotel Ratna Baru, Jl Sentani Raya, tel: (0967) 592 277.
Hotel Semeru, Jl Yabaso, tel: (0967) 591547.
Minang Jaya Hotel, Jl. Bisteur post Sentani, tel: (0967) 591067.

Merauke
Hotel Nirmala, Jl Raya Mandala 66, tel: (0971) 321849.
Hotel Megaria, Jl Raya Mandala 166, tel: (0971) 321932.
Hotel Asmat, Jl Trikora 3, tel: (0971) 321065.

Wamena
Baliem Valley Resort, tel: (0969) 32240, www.baliem-valley-resort.de   Luxury resort. Can organize tours treks.
Hotel Anggrek, Jl Ambon, Wamena, tel: (0969) 31242. Near the airport. Pleasant. Ask about staying in a **Dani village**. The **Lauk Inn** is a simple guesthouse in **Yiwika** popular with independent travellers (*'lauk'* means 'hello').

Biak
Good eating at stalls in the night market between the Garuda office and Penginapan Solo, with excellent fresh tuna. **Restaurant 99** (**'Sembilan Puluh Sembilan'**), Jl Iman Bonjol, is well-kept with an air-conditioned dining-room. **Rumah Makan Salam Manis** (also on Jl Iman Bonjol) is simple but with good food.

Jayapura
The Hawaii, Jl Irian 2, and the restaurant at the **Hotel Matoa** have a good range of dishes. There is excellent fresh-grilled fish at the night market along Jl Irian (ask for *ikan bakar*). The **Restoran Makassar** (in front of the Yasmin Hotel) also does good grilled fish.

Sentani
Yougwa is on the lake, with a good variety of food.

Wamena
There's a range of restaurants here serving food from around Indonesia. At the popular **Mas Budi** ask for the local speciality, huge crayfish. **Mentari**, Jl Yos Sudarso 46, is also good.

In **Jayapura** the Madinah Art Shop on Jl Perikanan is worth a look. There are several art/souvenir shops in **Hamadi**. In the **Baliem Valley** seek stone axes, cowrie-shell necklaces, string bags, penis gourds and woven baskets. Papua has a thriving illegal bird trade; please don't buy any bird-of-paradise skins.

The Papua office of **Adventure Indonesia** is at Jl Trikora 2, Wamena, www.@ adventureindonesia.com or join a tour from the Baliem Valley Resort.
Biak Diving, Jl Imam Bonjol 11a, tel: (0981) 26017, runs dive tours around Biak.

Travel Tips

Tourist Information

The best way to find up-to-date travel information on Indonesia is via the Internet. Some useful websites are given below. Otherwise, just type in the name of any place in Indonesia, however obscure, and be amazed at how many sites appear. Indonesia has entered the information age with enthusiasm! www.indonesia tourism.com and www.tourismindonesia.com are both quite good.

www.yellowpages.co.id – this is helpful for tel/fax numbers for hotels and other businesses.

www.baliadvisor.com, www.bali-blog.com and www.bali-paradise.com all have helpful information on hotels, attractions, activities etc in Bali.

www.yogyes.com – all kinds of information on Yogyakarta.

www.lombok-network.com – good for Lombok.

www.indonesia.embassy homepage.com and www.indonesia-ottawa.org are – excellent Indonesian embassy websites (London and Canada respectively) with all kinds of good information and links.

www.wtg-online.com – good for travel advice, public holidays, useful addresses.

www.expat.or.id – very useful for people planning a longer stay.

There has been a dramatic improvement in hotel provision in the last ten years, with various chains putting good hotels in even remote provincial towns (e.g. Novotel, Ibis, Sahid, Swiss-Belhotel). Entering the name of a particular chain will bring up the website. Some excellent little enterprises are also promoting themselves through the Web. A tiny selection of what is available is given below.

www.ecolodgesindonesia.com – several small, good quality guesthouses are described here.

www.nihiwatu.com – website for upmarket hideaway hotel on Sumba which has won awards for its environmental and social policies.

www.rosaecolodge.com – small boutique hotel offering tours of Baluran National Park, in East Java.

www.kaliandra.or.id – comfortable guesthouses set on a hill amidst woodland and valleys in East Java, an hour from Surabaya.

www.komodonationalpark.org – information on a national park run under an innovative management regime involving the park authorities and local people.

Entry Documents

Any visitor to Indonesia must ensure that their passport is valid for at least six months from their time of arrival. Visitors from many countries can obtain a visa on arrival in Indonesia. In 2007 these were most of the EU countries, the USA, Australia, New Zealand,

and some South American and Middle Eastern countries. Passport-holders from other ASEAN countries do not need a visa at all. If in doubt, check with your nearest Indonesian consulate or on the website of the Indonesian Embassy in Canada (as above).

The Visa On Arrival ('VOA') will allow you to stay for up to a month. For longer stays, you either have to leave the country for a night or two (a quick trip to Singapore will do) or get a visa in advance from an Indonesian con-sulate, which normally requires a letter of sponson-ship. If you are over 55 you can get a (fairly expensive) 'retirement visa' which allows you to stay for up to a year.

If you inted travelling to remote regions (especially Papua) take a few passport-size photos with you.

Customs

These are reasonably relaxed on the way into Indonesia though they can be pretty stiff when you are returning to your own home country because of fears of the Southeast Asian drugs trade. On entry into Indonesia there are reasonable allowances for tobacco, drink, perfume, etc. Drugs are banned so if you need to take medicine of any kind with you make sure that you have also a note from your doctor. Be careful about the souvenirs you buy. Many endangered species of wildlife are openly traded (albeit illegally) but could land you in trouble if you try to bring them home – for instance turtle shells and bird-of-paradise feathers.

Health Requirements

It is essential that you carry comprehensive health insurance. The Indonesian authorities are relaxed about health documentation. You should check the latest advice with your GP's surgery, and depending on where you plan to go, you should consider immunization against various serious diseases: particularly hepatitis, paratyphoid, and typhoid. If you plan to trek or go into remote areas and stay in budget accommodation, take tetanus, polio and tuber-culosis boosters to bring your cover up to date. Malaria is present in some areas so, depending on advice, take appropriate anti-malarials before you leave and remember to complete the programme. Expatriates living in Jakarta and elsewhere on Java and Bali do not bother with anti-malarial tablets. Make sure you cover up in the evenings, and buy an effective mosquito repellent.

Air Travel

This is the easiest and most comfortable mode of trans-port for most journeys in Indonesia, especially given the revolution in air travel and fares which has taken place over the last few years. The main international airport is Sukarno-Hatta International Airport (Jakarta);

others are Polonia (Medan), Ngurah Rai (Bali) and Juanda (Surabaya), but there are many others which permit international entry.

Domestic services: The main airlines are Garuda Indonesia (which operates also to international destinations) and Merpati Nusantara. There are also at least a dozen low-cost carriers operating more limited routes – up-to-date information on these can only be guaranteed on the spot, since they are prone to sud-den disappearance due to bankruptcy. The safety stan-dard of some of these smaller airlines is doubtful.

Road Travel

In Indonesia road traffic drives on the left (at least, it is supposed to). Most drivers of cars and motorbikes in Indonesia do not hold insurance. Except for public buses, minibuses, metered taxis and car hire, you have to bargain beforehand for all road journeys.

Car and bike hire: There are various car-hire companies in and around the major population centres, among them firms familiar to Western travellers, such as Avis. You should only consider driving a car yourself in Bali or Lombok, where traffic is reasonably well behaved, unless you speak Indonesian, are familiar with Asian road etiquette, and have strong nerves and fast reactions. It is much better to hire a car with a driver, which can be done for a reasonable rate.

In Bali and Lombok you can hire a motorbike. In many areas motorcycle taxis (called *ojeks*) operate for distances of up to 10km (6 miles) or so where there is no public transport – you will see groups of men hanging around on street corners or at special shelters on their motorbikes, with an extra helmet for the passenger. These are a cheap and efficient method of getting around – choose an older driver for safety. Bicycles can be hired in some places, notably Yogyakarta.

Licences: An International Driver's Licence is required if you want to rent a car or motorbike.

Taxis: These are available in most of the larger population centres, but outside the major towns they are unmetered: you have to bargain for the price of your journey before you set off. All registered taxis and hire cars have yellow number plates, with black for privately owned and red for state-owned vehicles. There are taxi ranks at all airports. You will be approached by unlicensed taxi drivers as you arrive at the airport, but only agree to go with one of these if you are certain of the price you should be paying. At Sukarno-Hatta (and elsewhere in Jakarta), look for the Golden Bird and Silver Bird taxi ranks – these are the best taxis, and the drivers often speak a little English.

Most other taxi drivers have limited or no English and may not know the loca-tions of any but the major thoroughfares.

Buses: Bus services vary from island to island. In Java there are numerous services between the major popula-tion centres. The best buses are those for longer journeys which have air conditioning, reclining seats and 'in-flight' films.

Minibuses: These are variously called *bemos*, *oplets*, colts or other local names. These vehicles are primarily for journeys between city centres and sub-urbs or provincial towns and villages and can seat up to about 10 people (although often they carry many more than this). Their big advan-tages are that they are cheap, they will let you off wherever along the route you want to go, and you get an interesting take on Indonesian life; the disadvantages are that they are uncomfortable and journeys are slow.

Horse-drawn carts and *becaks*: Horse-drawn carts are available in some towns and cities, operating rather like taxis; they can carry 2–4 passengers. A *becak* (pro-nounced 'baychak') is a tri-cycle whose driver pedals behind you; they can sometimes take two Indonesian passengers – but normally only one Westerner! As with horse-drawn carts, they are becoming rare in larger cities, but you may be able to find one in the suburbs or in the tourist areas.

CONVERSION CHART

From	To	Multiply By
Millimetres	Inches	0.0394
Metres	Yards	1.0936
Metres	Feet	3.281
Kilometres	Miles	0.6214
Square kilometres	Square miles	0.386
Hectares	Acres	2.471
Litres	Pints	1.760
Kilograms	Pounds	2.205
Tonnes	Tons	0.984

To convert Celsius to Fahrenheit: x 9 ÷ 5 + 32

Trains

Train services run only in Java and parts of Sumatra, and in some cases offer the best option for travelling between two places, particularly if you are able to choose one of the day-time trains which allow you to admire the country-side. The style of travel varies between luxury and rigour. Travel in Executive/Business class for spacious seats, civil fellow-passengers, and waiter service (some meals are included in the fare). Night trains run between Jakarta and Surabaya, with some trains running south via Yogyakarta and Solo and some along the north coast via Semarang. It is worth taking the train (the journey from Jakarta to Bandung is good) because of the views, but many of the swifter services run at night. With any rail journey, prepare for lengthy delays. Schedules and fares can be viewed at www.infoka.kereta-api.com

Sea Travel

There are state-run services serving all Indonesia's main ports; luxury accommodation (complete with en-suite bathrooms and in-cabin television) is available on these vessels, which are air condi-tioned and carry 1000–1500 people. There are numerous privately owned ferries – some taking cars, others for passen-gers only – between the various islands, covering short to long distances; on many comfort is at a premium. The schedules of the state-owned passenger line, Pelni, can be found at www.pelni.co.id

About 2000 traditional-style Bugis *pinisi* schooners still run between the islands, and for the adventure of a lifetime it is possible to travel on one of these. Do not expect comfort or punctilious arrival times. These boats are primarily trading vessels, and not much has changed about them for centuries – they still operate under sail, although they also have an engine.

Clothes: What to Pack

Indonesia's heat and dense humidity make it essential to pack a suitable range of light-weight clothing made from natural fibres, including a hat for protection against the sun. At the same time, remember that many of the sites you may wish to visit are at altitude and can be rather cold at night, so take a fleece or a warm sweat-shirt/jumper (also useful for over-fierce air conditioning in transport and hotels). A robust pair of lightweight trousers is a good idea for any jungle trekking or walking – for which you should also bring good trainers.

Large parts of Indonesia are Muslim, so women in par-ticular should err on the side of modesty when selecting their clothing. Indonesians of any religion are offended by scruffy or revealing clothing. Bikinis are permissible only on beach-es in tourist areas; elsewhere, bring a one-piece costume or, better still, swim in a T-shirt and shorts as local holiday-makers do. Shorts, halters and tank tops should be reserved for the beach or other sports facilities; miniskirts aren't acceptable except in Jakarta. Men should likewise pay some heed to modesty, certainly in the evenings; a shirt and long trousers is acceptable for almost everything. Bring a light jacket and tie if you are likely to be involved in more formal occasions.

Money Matters

The Indonesian currency unit is the rupiah (Rp). In late 2007 there were 18,800 Rupiah to £1. Coins are Rp100 and Rp500, while notes are Rp1000, Rp5000, Rp10,000, Rp20,000 and Rp 50,000. When getting money from the bank ask for smaller denomi-nation notes, since it can sometimes be hard to change Rp 50,000 ones (although the rate of inflation is such that using larger denomination notes is now easier).

Money is worth a lot more in Indonesia than you may be accustomed to: the cost of living is very cheap, although in tourist areas restaurants etc. will charge prices close to European ones. **Currency exchange:** Normal banking hours are 08:00–14:30 Monday–Friday and 08:00–12:00 on Saturday, although branches of banks located in hotels may keep longer hours. Banks will take travellers' cheques, American Express being the preferred variety; you can expect to take about 15 minutes over the transaction. You often get a better rate of exchange at money-changers, and it's quicker too! Your hotel cashier will also be able to exchange foreign currency, although the rates will be very poor. A set fee is charged for each transaction, so it is best to opt for a large sum each time. If you are changing foreign currency bills, you will get a poorer exchange rate if the note is crumpled, dirty, or has writing on it – or they may not accept them at all.

ATMs (Automatic Teller Machines) are widespread at airports and throughout towns, so you can withdraw cash from your home bank account in local currency for a better exchange rate than you get from banks or money-changers – beware of steep charges for withdrawing small amounts, though.

Credit cards and travellers' cheques: Credit cards are not widely used in Indonesia outside the major population centres. Avoid using them except at reputable hotels, supermarkets, etc., because of the possibilities for fraud.

Tipping: The bigger hotels usually add a 21% tax and service charge; otherwise (if you're happy with the service) you can add 5–10% to your bills. Taxi drivers need not be tipped, but do round up to the nearest Rp5000. Hire-car drivers expect more. Porters (e.g. at the airport) should be offered at least Rp5000 per bag, depending on the size/weight of the bag.

Business Hours

Offices are usually open either from 08:00–16:00 or 09:00–17:00, with a lunch break from 12:00–13:00; these hours operate Monday– Friday and, if applicable, Saturday. Government offices throughout Indonesia are open 08:00–16:00, Monday– Friday.

Shopping hours are generally 09:00–21:00 for the supermarkets and department stores in the larger population centres, with truncated opening hours on Sundays. In the lesser cities and towns the shops are often closed from 13:00–17:00.

The opening hours of museums and galleries, and also the starting times of traditional dance performances, are displayed in local information centres. This also applies to temple ceremonies in Bali and main tourist centres in Java. Many museums are closed on Mondays.

Time

Sumatra, Java, West Kalimantan and Central Kalimantan are 7 hours ahead of GMT; East Kalimantan, South Kalimantan, Sulawesi, Bali and Nusa Tenggara are 8 hours ahead of GMT; and Maluku and Papua are 9 hours ahead of GMT.

Postage

Postage overseas is fairly expensive, although some larger items can be shipped home for a reasonable sum. Any valuable item being posted should always be

registered. *Kilat* (meaning lightning) is an inexpensive Express Postal service which also works for international mail.

Communications

The Internet has taken off all over Indonesia and you will find Internet cafés ('Warnet') in most towns. Main post offices in the capitals host the Post Office's Wasantara Net Service.

Electricity

Most places use 220–240 volts/50 cycles AC. Plugs are of the two-pronged European kind. The electricity supply is fairly reliable (although brown-outs are not uncommon). If you are staying in budget accommodation, it is a good idea to carry a spare 60 watt lightbulb (with screw fitting) to substitute for the dim ones usually found in hotels.